PERSEVERANCE

PRINCIPLES

JJ MAZZO

PERSEVERANCE
PRINCIPLES

HOW TO UNLOCK
CONFIDENCE,
CONSISTENCY,
AND WEALTH
UNDER PRESSURE

WILEY

Published by John Wiley & Sons, Inc., Hoboken, New Jersey.
Published simultaneously in Canada.

For general information on our other products and services or for technical support, please contact our Customer Care Department within the United States at (800) 762-2974, outside the United States at (317) 572-3993 or fax (317) 572-4002.

Wiley also publishes its books in a variety of electronic formats. Some content that appears in print may not be available in electronic formats. For more information about Wiley products, visit our web site at www.wiley.com.

Library of Congress Cataloging-in-Publication Data is Available:

ISBN 9781394377527 (Cloth)
ISBN 9781394377534 (ePub)
ISBN 9781394377541 (ePDF)

Cover Design: Wiley
Cover Image: Colors Hunter - Chasseur de Couleurs/Getty Images
Printed and bound by CPI Group (UK) Ltd, Croydon, CR0 4YY

C9781394377527_120825

To my wife, Kimberly,

My partner, my person, the love of my life. Your grace in the chaos, strength through every storm, and steady belief have been my anchor. You've stood beside me through every setback and every step forward—never wavering, always lifting. This journey, and everything built along the way, is because of your quiet resilience and relentless love. I love you more than words can hold.

To my daughters, Brooklyn and London,

This book is for you—and because of you. You are my greatest joy and the reason I keep climbing. Watching you grow into strong, kind, and fearless young women has taught me what perseverance truly means. You remind me daily that the hard path is always worth it. I love you with everything I am—and everything I hope to be.

Contents

Foreword

As the founder of a mortgage company, I've had the opportunity to meet hundreds—maybe thousands—of people trying to make a name for themselves in this business. Some show up polished, with résumés and degrees. Others show up with hunger and hustle. But every so often, someone shows up with something different—a raw drive not just to succeed, but to *transform*. That was JJ.

I still remember the first time I met him. His flight had been canceled during a total blackout at the Atlanta airport. Most people would've called it quits, rescheduled, maybe used it as an excuse to avoid a tough meeting. Not JJ. He found a way—literally showed up in clothes from Walmart, shorts, and a T-shirt, ready to go. That told me all I needed to know about him: this was someone who made things happen, no matter the obstacles.

Let me be clear—JJ didn't walk into this world with a silver spoon. Far from it. He didn't come from money and had the chips staked against him. We're talking real setbacks—sleeping in his car, family hardship, and more. But what impressed me most wasn't just that he turned things around. It's that he *kept* turning things around—relentlessly, purposefully, and with heart.

Early on, JJ made it clear that he wasn't just working to survive—he was working to build something bigger. He was in full pursuit of financial independence and knew he couldn't get there alone. He's completely coachable and has found good role models and mentors. When we met, he wasn't just looking for a job, he was looking to be coached. And that's a key distinction. JJ didn't want handouts or shortcuts. He wanted guidance, structure, and accountability. And when he found someone who could give him that, he locked in. He listened. He applied. And he evolved—fast.

I've been in this business a long time, and I've met all kinds of people—the polished execs, the legacy kids, the ones who've had a playbook handed to them. JJ's not one of those. He's what I call a nontraditional leader. He's raw, real, and 100% coachable. And because of that, he's become one of the most thoughtful, driven, and accountable professionals I know—in or out of our industry.

Perseverance Principles isn't just about financial independence—though JJ's journey there is impressive. It's about grit. It's about perseverance with purpose. And it's about how anyone—regardless of where they start, can become something extraordinary with the right mindset and the right people around them.

JJ's story proves that where you begin doesn't define where you end up. He found mentors and clung to them like glue. He made hard choices. He changed—not just his income, but his health, his mindset, and how he shows up for the people around him. I know, because I've watched him do it—and I've felt the impact personally. JJ still strives to improve himself every single day.

If you're someone who thinks you're too far behind to catch up, or if you've ever looked at someone successful and thought, "Why not me?"—read this book. JJ won't give you easy answers, but will give you the truth. And maybe, just maybe, the fire to start your own transformation.

—Ron Leonhardt
CEO, CrossCountry Mortgage

The Why
Blasting Through Your Barriers

Adversity teaches us a lot about ourselves. When we're challenged, we often grow and change to become better versions of who we are.

Unfortunately, many of these challenges are thrown at us, and we have little say whether to accept them or not. They simply enter our lives, and we have no choice but to take them on the best way we know how.

At other times, our challenges are created by self-inflicted wounds and poor behavior we direct at ourselves. This can result from a lack of confidence, poor self-esteem, or feeling trapped in a situation where we see no way out.

We lose hope and forget that the best versions of ourselves come at the price of fighting for who we want to be.

As you'll read in *Perseverance Principles*, I've lived through all these things. Some of those were piled on me by my family members and work colleagues. Others I'm directly responsible for, such as committing crimes, long-term drug and alcohol abuse, being a terrible husband and father at times, and financial ruin on more than one occasion. I could easily make the case that I should have died, wound up in prison, or lived a life of poverty and destitution.

But I'm still here. I survived because I found a way to persevere.

I've thought long and hard about how and why I survived some pretty horrific chapters in my life, and I'm not telling you my story because I want your sympathy. I don't want a hug, nor do I want you to see me as a victim because I don't see myself that way. Nothing could be further from why I'm about to tell you about my past.

This also isn't a contest to see who wins the prize for the most trauma in their lives. Although I've been through some difficult challenges, Lord knows others have me beat. It's my way of opening up your eyes to how tough *you* really are and using that toughness to create a better life for you and your family.

While some of *Perseverance Principles* is about how I first learned to survive and later thrive, it's even more critical for you to understand this: after everything I went through—and found a way to turn things around—*you* can too.

I don't know you personally, but I know you've gone through tough times too. We all do. That's the price you pay for being a part of the human race. In that way, we're alike. And from that, you and I have a bond. I want to use that bond to help you better understand how to use your tough times and why proving you can persevere.

To do this, I've structured this book as a journey. Each of the seven principles I explore is intertwined, just like life itself. I believe that, like me, to understand better how to persevere and ultimately live a better life, you'll encounter these seven principles at one point or another.

Fighting Through Your Discomfort Zone

Developing Self-Leadership

Putting Plans into Practice

Tapping into a Support System

Stacking Consistent Wins

Creating Financial Security

Building the Road to Your Legacy

I've put them in a business context when it's possible because my success in the business world in recent years has centered around my ability to work through these principles and ultimately persevere in my personal and professional life.

However, I've also explained them in a way that works no matter what you want to accomplish in life. Your journey will be different than mine, and your timetable will also differ. What matters is that you find wisdom in my words and then take the necessary steps to blast through uncomfortable truths about who you are so that you can focus on who you were meant to be.

It's not easy, and it's not linear. You will confront your demons as I have confronted mine. I still grapple with them often, but I'm better armed with the tools and strategies I need to minimize the dark parts of my past that I allowed to rule over me for a long time.

Much of this is because I relied on my Christian faith and decided early on that while I might have been suffering in many ways, nobody would outwork me. I poured myself into my work and faith in God to turn my life around.

I did not give up once I set my mind to it, and that's a big part of what I want to instill in you. I want to inspire you, give you hope, make you think and reflect on your life so far, and give you what you need to find a higher degree of happiness that eludes many other people.

As you learn more about me, it's possible you will see my life reflected in your own. Some of you have been through worse than I have. Your story will be different than mine, but we're all linked by common challenges in many ways.

The best place for us to start is for me to be real and reveal many of the tough times I've faced. Once I tell you how I persevered, I hope I'll gain your respect for how far I've come and, more importantly, how far *you* can potentially travel down the road meant for you.

Hard Lessons

My childhood ended when I was six years old.

I was exposed to things no child should go through. I had no choice at the time. As I grew into an adult, I realized staying in a dark place was a choice I made even when I had other options.

It was part of a hard reality check many years later as I started to understand the impact those past traumas had on me. When I was young, I was stuck in a generational cycle of dysfunction. Without a clear understanding of what was going on, I wasn't equipped to break free from the only life I knew. So I persevered, surviving the best way I knew how.

At that age and for many years that followed, I didn't understand much about all the things I've been through. I didn't comprehend that I was persevering through some really bad things life had thrown at me.

I was just hanging on. For me, as early as I can remember, it was all about surviving the best way I could, given the events and circumstances of my life, some of which I'm going to tell you about now.

The sheer amount of what I've been through may blow you away. I know this because it blows me away when I think about it, and I already know all the details! As incredible as some of it may sound, every word is true. And much of it is painful to recount. Ironically, I accepted it and thought it was no big deal for a long time.

I'm letting you into my life because I want you to listen and understand that if I survived all I've been through, you can too. Think of this as my résumé and interview applying for the job of perseverance expert. Ultimately, you'll decide if I'm qualified to tell you what I know about perseverance.

If you've never experienced overwhelming trauma like I have, and you've led a pretty good life, you've still faced setbacks and challenges because *everyone* faces setbacks and challenges. It's the nature of life. You've persevered in your way, and your struggles shouldn't be discounted because you never came from an abusive or broken home, faced financial ruin, or dealt with substance abuse or mental health issues. However, as bad as I had it, I realize that some of you also had it much worse.

I believe there is a lot more to your life and mine on pages that haven't been written yet. Some of it will be good and some will be bad. We have no choice but to face these things, and being armed with the best tools and strategies is the key to writing the best possible story.

In this way, what separates us is much less than what makes us all the same.

Do you understand what I'm saying? We're all the same.

I think once you hear more about who I am and what I've been through, including years and years of amazing therapy, I hope to convince you that I am more than qualified to help you. I sincerely want to guide you through your battles and your stories of perseverance.

Dreams and Downward Spirals

I didn't have big dreams of becoming a loan officer when I was younger. In fact, other than dreams of being wealthy, as most of us have, I'm not sure I had any dreams at all. Dreams are all about possibilities and going on offense to find the life you love. Unfortunately, when I was younger, I played defense for as long as I can remember.

Throughout my early years, there was never a comforting blanket of security I could wrap myself in.

My dad was originally from South Philly before he left his wife at the time and his daughter, who is also my half-sister. He moved to Southern California, where he hustled at everything from fencing stolen goods to running a brothel and smuggling drugs from Mexico. He was a selfish and narcissistic man at times who had a rough life growing up, so rough was all he knew.

He met my mom on a double date swap in Beverly Hills. Dad had a way with the ladies, often dressing nice, meeting women, and finding ways to make them pay for a night out on the town instead of him. They fell in with each other for what can best be described as an interesting relationship.

They got married in 1976, and they each had children from previous relationships, so I became the youngest of five children. By the time I was born, my half-brothers and half-sister were already at least 15 years older than me.

My mom reformed my dad to some degree. He got into furniture sales, design, and marketing; this was the dad I knew and loved very much. However, as I later learned, he was also the man who gave one of my siblings cocaine for the first time when that sibling was just 19.

I mentioned that my childhood ended when I was six. How do I know this? Because that's when I first started therapy after experiencing early trauma. I was unruly, even at an early age, because of it, and my mom did her best to brush it under the rug. But because of this disconnection between what I felt and what was acknowledged, I was confused about my childhood for decades.

Shortly after that, my mom finally had enough when she found out my dad had another woman on the side, which some might consider a mistress, but it was tough to put a label on that relationship. My dad left, and my mom turned bitter. She gave plenty of things to my brothers but not me, leaving me confused and hurt. As I learned later, it was because I had a pretty good relationship with my dad despite his shortcomings. For decades, she never told me she was proud of me or gave me kudos because my mom always saw my dad when she looked at me.

Growing up, we never owned a home. My mom and dad were constantly moving from one town to the next because my dad was always chasing work. In fact, we were at the far end of the spectrum and moved more than 10 times before I was 16 years old, often living in a hotel, just trying to survive.

Many times, when my dad gave a landlord the first and last month's rent, I always joked it was probably the only money the landlord would see while we lived there.

Constantly moving meant I went to a lot of different schools, and it was always a crapshoot as to how I would fit in. More often than not, I found it hard to make friends because I believed I was never good enough to fit in at school. Struggling to make new friends was a constant battle for years, made worse by the fact that I was bullied from the time I was 8 until I turned 15.

I sucked my thumb until I was seven because I was so insecure. I was a gangly young kid with a big head, my teeth sticking out in all directions, and a bad case of acne. I tried to dress decently enough to avoid being mocked in school. The one thing I had going for me was that I was a driven kid, but not very scholastic. I was hyper and had trouble concentrating. But in a weird way, I was lucky because things didn't come easily to me in school. I had to fight for everything I got.

Eventually, I did what a lot of kids in my situation do. I turned to drugs. I became a stoned, angry teenager who smoked weed, drank, and dropped *a lot* of acid. I couldn't physically escape my world, so I mentally escaped the only way I knew how, by getting high to dull my pain.

In time, my bad behavior caught up with me. When I was 13, I stole my parents' car and was arrested. I was punished by being sent to an all-boys boarding school in rural New Hampshire. As a skate-boarding kid from SoCal, to say that I was probably the most out-of-place kid in New England would not be much of a stretch. To make matters worse, I almost got kicked out for stealing. I survived that episode, but just barely.

I went back to California changed but not reformed. That's because boarding school added more trauma to what was already there. So, it didn't take long before I slipped back into my old ways. Unfortunately, I was older now and had even more opportunities to get myself into deeper trouble. Over those years, I bounced around several high schools and became so difficult to deal with that my mom kicked me out of the house when I was 18, although my brothers stayed at home into their forties.

Faced with the prospect of being out on my own and with a lot of troublesome baggage I was lugging around, I turned to DJing in clubs and at raves across the country, which I had gotten into after returning from boarding school. I also worked part-time at an EDM record store to put a few more bucks in my pocket and stay as close as possible to music.

But the biggest thing that happened is that I began working in the mortgage industry right around this time. I was all about the hustle and the money, and this sounded like it could satisfy both of those things. It turned out to be divine intervention, but I didn't recognize it until much later.

I worked my ass off. Driven to prove everyone wrong about who they thought I was, I poured myself into all three jobs. I worked from 8 a.m. to 6 p.m. Monday through Friday at my mortgage job, then hustled off to my record store job working from 7 to 10 p.m. four days a week. And on weekends, I'd squeeze in some DJ gigs, typically on Saturdays, often not going on until 2 a.m.

Driven by Denial, Survival, and Anger

So many emotions fueled my life in those early days. I was driven by the need to simply survive. Eventually, that became more complicated by a lot of unresolved anger that had built up over my childhood. Although that anger continued to gnaw at me and drag me down, I also used it as motivation to become an unstoppable force.

I decided that since nobody was coming to save me, I would have to save myself. In a word, I overcompensated. On the surface, I was highly successful. I quickly moved my way up from delivering home inspections to becoming a loan officer assistant to junior loan officer and eventually into operations and sales management in my early twenties.

Lots of people get into the mortgage industry and make big money. I'm no exception, but because my scars ran deeper than most, I had an extra level of motivation to do well. I realized that the harder I worked, the more I made, which meant I was finally in control of my future—or so I thought.

Although I was relentless, I'd love to tell you that I was driven by my desire to be the best version of myself. But the truth is, I was driven by a need to be seen and my heartfelt desire to hear someone tell me they were proud of me. I wanted to feel that I was good enough for once in my life.

I was also outwardly successful, making enough money to buy a home and later start a family. Inside, I was persevering because I couldn't overcome feeling emotionally empty. To make matters worse, I continued to feed that emptiness with huge amounts of alcohol, weed, and cocaine.

You name it, and I was doing it while also working 80 hours a week, living paycheck to paycheck, no matter how much I made.

The logical question is, how could I work that many hours and still barely get by?

Easy. Because as fast as I was making money, I was spending it like my dad had taught me, as I watched him spend his money. My dad always thought he could make more money as needed, until the time came when he couldn't.

I knew how to make money, but I didn't know how to keep it. I was so messed up that I kept trying to fill a bottomless hole with money and drugs in hopes that it would help me mask and bury a lifetime of pain.

Although I was out on my own, there were still lots of challenges going on with my family, ranging from serious health and financial issues to changing family dynamics that were an endless cycle of pain, shame, and confusion for me. The harder I worked to prove people wrong and distance myself from these things, the more I had to mask my feelings to remain functional in a highly demanding profession.

I hid those feelings by pouring myself into my work, doing everything I could to prove to my mom and others that they were wrong. If I were supposed to meet 20 Realtors in a week, I would make it a point to meet 40. When it was time to make 20 cold calls for the day, I'd make 100 of them. Part of this was driven by wanting to be financially successful, but another agenda existed.

I struggled on the inside, but I felt duty bound to honor my family by working hard. My wife never stopped loving and believing in me, and to this day, Kimberly has stayed by my side and put up with a lot more than she should have through all of our ups and downs. In that way, I'm one of the luckiest men in the world because I'd be lost or possibly dead without her or my children.

Ultimately, I promised myself that I would never give up and would continually improve. That determination never went away and, in many ways, is the core definition of perseverance.

It stayed with me even when I went from earning about $200,000 a year to $2 million a year in just two years. But because success is never a straight line, it also stayed with me when I failed miserably.

I had hoped my work would save me, and it did. But as you might guess, this could only go on for so long. And eventually, it stopped working for me. I crashed, and it was not a soft landing.

Over the next several years, Kimberly and I endured one catastrophe after another. My mom, whom I never reconciled with, and the brother I was closest to passed away. Our home was foreclosed. We filed for bankruptcy. I got fired, and we found ourselves living in poverty yet again.

Kimberly's mom passed away from a heart attack, and my dad got sick and spent two months in an ICU. Although he recovered well enough to come home, I shouldered the responsibility of taking care of him for the rest of his life before he passed away from dementia.

To make matters worse, I continued to suffer from massive depression, anxiety, and thoughts of suicide. I was privately struggling at a time when I had a three-year-old, a newborn girl, and Kimberly at home, counting on me.

Despite all this, I hadn't reached the bottom yet, which I'll tell you about in the next chapter.

All these things severely impacted my young family. When you're in the middle of it, like I was then, you don't fully see it as a generational cycle you need to break, but that's precisely what was happening. Realizing I needed to break free from my past wouldn't come until much later.

Unfortunately, stories like mine are common in business. We often know how to earn a payday for ourselves, but because we're constantly trying to prove our worth, we fall into the trap of seeking validation and recognition. We fall back on our comfortable but dangerous vices when we don't get it. And in the end, after working our asses off, we have nothing to show for it.

Despite all I've been through, I'm still alive, scars and all. There's *a lot* more I could have told you about, but I think I've told you enough to make my point without turning this into another therapy session for me.

In the end, after I crawled out of all these minefields, I asked myself one important question.

What have my experiences taught me?

A Common Bond

Every person has it in them to persevere. In that way, we are all well-informed on the challenges of perseverance to one degree or another.

Like so many of you, since I was born, my life has been challenging in ways that defy the norm. I have encountered extremes in my family and business life that came close to killing me more than once. I hope you haven't gone through such extremes as I have. But if you have, you must go easy on yourself and be kind to the person you are today. Where there's life, there is hope, and that's what you must focus on while you continue to persevere in your own way.

However, becoming someone who relies on perseverance to survive also means learning better ways of living. It's about not tolerating the cards you've been dealt. It's about finding inner strength through self-belief and a greater reliance on faith to find better hands to play.

There is no single best way to persevere because your challenges differ from mine. However, we all share many things in common when it comes to making ourselves more resilient and open to change, and those are the things I want to tell you about in a lot more detail. When you connect with the perseverance principles I've laid out, I hope it will create a clearer path to a better life for you.

So, if you're ready, let's start together at the beginning by fighting through your discomfort zone.

1

Fighting Through Your Discomfort Zone

Children are often the biggest casualties of their parents' struggling or failed relationship. As I've told you, that was the case with my parents. Their lies, fighting, distrust, and other problems undermined the stability of our entire family for years. I was so young when these things started that I just assumed that's how families were.

Of course, I was completely wrong, never realizing that while all families face challenges, we were outliers in every sense of the word.

When parents ultimately decide to go their separate ways, as my parents did, there is a sense of relief, but much of the toxic anger that fueled the split often remains. In some cases, with nothing left to lose, bitterness rears its ugly head, and things get worse.

In my case, while my parents were together, I had a pretty good relationship with my dad. I looked up to him despite his flaws, as boys often do. My mom, who gave selflessly to do what she could to find normalcy, built emotional walls to counter the horrible situation she found herself in.

The dysfunction that had taken place for years gradually overcame my mom. Her indifference grew so intense that, right or wrong, much of it was directed at me over time. I don't know if she stopped loving me, but the way she loved me definitely changed. Consumed by my dad's betrayal, she unleashed her anger and punished me every chance she could. I did the same thing to her, creating a vicious cycle.

When I saw her, she constantly berated me, told me I would never be successful, and drove my self-esteem into the ground. I was bewildered, crushed, and pissed off. That became a big reason why I turned to drugs, alcohol, and got into other kinds of trouble.

They continued with an on-again, off-again relationship until they finally got divorced when I was in my early twenties.

My dad's ways finally caught up with him. He had continued to see another woman behind my mother's back, which I didn't know at the time. I just knew that when their marriage dissolved, he ended up living on my couch for a while until I bought him a condo in New Jersey so he could start over.

I never really reconciled with my mother or my brothers before their deaths several years later, which I still regret. Right or wrong, they transferred my mom's hatred of my dad at the time and placed it squarely on me. I was victimized, and I never really knew why for the longest time. It turns out she was protecting me by never fully sharing some of the things my dad did. Those revelations didn't come until after I was well into my forties, so I carried around her opinions of me like a ton of dead weight for many years.

Despite a lot of emotional baggage, I promised to never give up. That overcompensating drive was a key reason I enjoyed success early in my career.

And because success is never linear, I refused to quit even when I hit rock bottom, as you're about to read.

Why You're Uncomfortable

Every person is a unique sum of their past experiences and relationships. Many people, including me, have been undermined in ways we don't fully recognize. We may not even be the slightest bit aware of those acts because they are ingrained in us from the time we were born and continue to stack up against us as we age.

Whether through abuse, neglect, abandonment, or other negative things that have happened to us, we have developed a fear-based fight-or-flight response that creates anger or defensiveness we may not understand. The sad truth is that when our early home life is challenging, it is often the reflection of generational cycles passed down to our parents, who, in many ways, are victims of the same pattern. Like us, our parents may not fully understand why they act the way they do. Often, it is all they've ever known.

One thing is for sure: pain begets pain. And when those who love you are dealing with their generational pain, they aren't always fully capable of making the best decisions that affect children in their care.

Nobody sets out to be a poor parent, but if what a parent has learned is flawed, that imprints on their parenting style and ultimately onto their children, who may recognize this at some point, but often when it is too late.

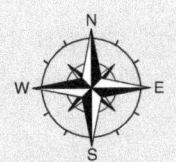

Respond to Failure

Failure happens to us whether we like it or not. However, when things don't go our way, we can choose how to respond. When we accept and learn from our failures, we grow. When we fight them, we become our worst enemy. Failures are one form of perseverance, and anyone who has ever become a champion understands they are an integral stepping stone to mastery. When we achieve mastery, our perseverance is rewarded, and our discomfort zone doesn't paralyze us in self-pity.

The result is that as we grow up, we have blind spots. These points of pain appear to exist for no good reason other than to create barriers to being the most fully realized version of ourselves. We know we should live a happier and fuller life, but we don't know how to get there. So we persevere, staying on the course we're on, hoping things will change and we'll eventually find the joy deep down we know we deserve.

We understand change must occur, but we're so afraid to fail that we don't have the courage to take a chance and break through those fears. We remain in our discomfort zone because even though it isn't where we want to be, we know what that zone feels like, and it provides a warped sense of safety for us.

If this sounds like you, you don't yet understand that your authentic self was never meant to live in fear, and that you deserve love and compassion instead.

A lifelong relationship with limiting beliefs is incredibly difficult to overcome. Pain planted by others is ugly and often invisible. But changing your mindset and getting new and better results is possible. Understand that persevering in your discomfort zone is not the only time or place you must hang tough. You must also persevere when looking inward, making choices, taking action, and giving these things as much time as needed to take effect.

That doesn't happen in a vacuum. You must also cope with your past and current state of affairs while simultaneously attempting to eliminate your discomfort zone. Your work, family, health, finances, relationships, and more must be maintained as you redefine what each will look like going forward. It's not easy, but *you* can do it if *you* want it bad enough.

But first, you'll need to deal with the biggest thing holding you back.

Your ego.

Hostage Negotiations with Your Ego

After everything I've been through, I've learned one undeniable fact.

Your ego's peak is where your life plateaus.

Everyone needs some degree of ego in their lives. Ego, when correctly managed, gives us confidence. As a leader, it creates a certain amount of swagger to help you sell common goals and an overall mission. Throughout time, ego has been an evolutionary necessity, protecting us from harsh realities that sometimes threaten our very survival.

However, an ego without appropriate guardrails is a huge impediment to progress. An oversized ego becomes an anesthetic that deadens us to reality. When this happens, our judgment is colored, and we risk looking like fools if we're out of touch with the truth.

Self-centered thinking can result in things taking longer than expected or in outcomes that may surprise us. When fighting your ego, you lose out to your short-term desires instead of the benefits of a more long-term, healthier approach.

A lot has been written about the challenges of an unhealthy ego.

For example, Dr. Robert Schuller once remarked, "Big egos have little ears."

Deepak Chopra offers the insight that "the ego relies on the familiar. It is reluctant to experience the unknown, which is the very essence of life."

Also, consider the words of Dr. Wayne Dyer, who said, "You can either be a host to God or a hostage to your ego. It's your call."

The unchecked ego is artificial, producing mental clutter, killing creativity, and stifling intuition. Left to its own devices, a cartoonish anvil wrapped around your neck weighs you down.

If you're in the mortgage industry or any other lucrative sales profession, it can be a highly profitable form of dysfunction. Just because you're making a lot of money doesn't mean you're not immune to the damage an unchecked ego can cause.

Ego makes you feel like you're in control when you're really not. Unless you're vigilant, your ego can overtake and push you further from your goals. It's a self-inflicted, destructive form of perseverance. And it's totally unnecessary.

How you find the right balance between ego and humility is as unique and individual as you are. The key is awareness of yourself and others, and who you want to be. Recognize when you fall into ego-driven habits and patterns. Your ego is in place to protect you by default, so you may not even be aware that you are engaging in a limiting belief or self-sabotaging behavior.

Curb those tendencies, and you'll clear a path out of your self-imposed discomfort zone. Your relationships will improve, and when you strip away your ego, you'll be left with a focused approach to accomplishing what you want most.

You may think your ego is protecting you, but in reality, it often only extends the perseverance required to get to where you want to go.

Take Dana White's story as an example.

Dana White and the Battle for Octagon Supremacy

Few people know the value of perseverance better than Ultimate Fighting Championship (UFC) mastermind Dana White. Many people know who he is now, but few know about his long, hard haul to the top. It's a classic story of perseverance with more than one visit to the discomfort zone, including running afoul of an Irish mob boss along the way.

White jumped into the fight game in Boston when he was still a teenager. Over the next 10 years, he grinded as a boxer, trainer, referee, gym manager, fight manager, and promoter, learning every part of the business as he went.

His reputation grew, and he started to attract a lot of clients at health clubs where he taught classes. But he also caught the attention of Whitey Bulger and his notorious Winter Hill Gang. Gang members visited White and his partner Peter Welsh one day and demanded a taste of the action, "billing" White $2,500 as their cut, which was still a lot of money for White at the time. When the gang stepped up their threats and backed Dana into a corner, he decided to leave Boston, landing in Las Vegas to start a new chapter in his life.

At the time, the UFC was a fledgling brand trying to carve out a niche as a disruptor in the fight business. White soon joined the UFC and quickly became a successful trainer. However, the unregulated nature of the sport didn't sit well in many quarters, and the UFC struggled financially after it was banned from pay-per-view bouts and in many arenas throughout the United States.

Although bankruptcy loomed, White believed in the future of the sport. When he learned the UFC was for sale, he called his friends, casino owners Lorenzo and Frank Fertitta, to bankroll the purchase of the UFC for $2 million. Together, they began a series of moves to regulate and bring legitimacy to the sport and cut deals in France, Germany, Mexico, and other countries to turn the UFC into a global powerhouse. It took several years, but it has grown to become the undisputed champion of the MMA world, with fights in 175 countries, 100+ training facilities, and a television viewing audience that has reached more than a billion households since its launch.

The Fertitta brothers eventually sold the UFC brand in 2016 for a whopping $4.025 billion, making it the biggest sports acquisition of all time. White stayed on as the UFC's president, and his share and net worth eventually grew to an estimated $500 million based on proceeds from the original sale plus a stake he received under the new ownership.

White could have completely folded when the Winter Hill Gang came to collect. Still, by pushing through a menacing discomfort zone and staying focused for more than two decades, he turned years of sweat and a $2,500 debt into a massive fortune in one of the great stories of contemporary business perseverance.

The Tale of the Two Implode-O-Meters

For those of you who aren't familiar with the mortgage lending industry, about 70% of all mortgages are funded by mortgage banks or nonbank lenders. These lenders differ from commercial banks like Chase or Bank of America because they only underwrite mortgage loans. They don't hold deposits or conduct business activities similar to banks.

They make most of their money by funding loans and then selling them off almost immediately for a premium, typically within days of funding a loan. Consistently turning loans like this is the lifeblood of a mortgage bank. If those lenders can't sell those loans profitably, they risk going under.

In times of uncertainty, mortgage lenders may be unable to sell a loan for several reasons, such as offering poor or risky terms and making it unattractive to a potential buyer like Fannie Mae or Wall Street investors. They may have held onto the loan too long in a rising rate environment or encountered less liquidity in the market because fewer investors want to buy loans.

If they can't move the loans, these lenders carry too much overhead and must eventually file for bankruptcy to get relief from their encumbered obligations. Most just close their doors.

Each of these factors played a role in 2006 when the systemic problems of the subprime segment of the mortgage lending industry turned into complete chaos. The problem was so bad that it caught the attention of an Emory University computer scientist named Aaron Krowne, who started a website late that year to track potentially failing lenders.

At that time, liquidity became a significant issue as many investors who had committed to buy loans from mortgage banks refused to follow through on their commitments. Using data culled from the Mortgage Bankers Association and aggregating news about failing subprime lenders, Krowne created quite a buzz when he launched the site.

He called his website the Implode-O-Meter.

During the height of the crisis, the Implode-O-Meter received as many as 100,000 daily visits. The site was also not shy about calling out significant mortgage banking institutions like Washington Mutual, or New Century Mortgage, which was the lifeline for many companies, including the one I worked for, creating turmoil in the entire industry.

The site was equally controversial and helpful because it warned people to avoid lenders or investors close to bankruptcy. As the site grew, it also became a forum for people in the industry to become whistleblowers who exposed corruption and fraud by some lenders.

As you might guess, that led to several lawsuits by disgruntled parties named on the Implode-O-Meter, and the site was temporarily shut down until those legal issues were adjudicated. However, the site reemerged, and as of 2024, it is still active. It has documented almost 400 mortgage banking closures since it first launched.

If you were in the mortgage banking industry post-2006, the mortgage industry was a potential nightmare scenario on many levels. The Implode-O-Meter drew massive attention to the subprime crisis, and many industry people, including me, checked the site several times a day to make sure our companies hadn't appeared. Unfortunately, one day, mine did.

More than once, as soon as a paycheck landed in my hands, I would run to the bank and cash it as quickly as possible to make sure it didn't bounce. In the end, many lives were ruined due to the subprime collapse, and all the survivors could do was persevere while that market segment eventually corrected itself.

People like me were also dealing with a lot of other things at the time, some of which I've already alluded to. The industry Implode-O-Meter was serious enough by itself, but I had my own Implode-O-Meter that I was facing as well.

Part of perseverance is about survival, and at the height of the Implode-O-Meter phenomenon, I was personally in a dark place, literally on life support for months on end. Discomfort doesn't even begin to describe how I felt because as the mortgage banking industry collapsed, so did everything I had worked for to that point. I kept asking myself if what I thought was my life's work would ever mean something or if my mom and others were right about me.

In short, I experienced my version of the Implode-O-Meter. While that experience came close to destroying me, I later realized it was exactly what needed to happen so that I could move beyond my discomfort zone and find a better life on the other side.

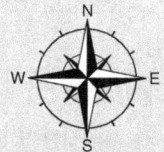

Refuse to Be a Victim

Refuse to be a victim. You have that choice. We can accept what is happening and use it for the good of growth, or grovel by blaming others to divert from our shortcomings. Many things will not go our way, but the lessons we learn from each other can point us in a positive direction that we can use later on. However, when we allow our ego to stand in the way of a necessary humbling process, we are slower to learn as we continue to swim against life's current. Lessons are constant, but how long we take to learn them is up to us.

Moving out of my discomfort zone meant I had to first go *through* my discomfort zone and my personal Implode-O-Meter. It started long before, but came to a head one memorable day at the height of the market crash in 2009. That's the day I heard a bad sound coming from my driveway.

I was already fighting anxiety, depression, and bankruptcy, and Kimberly and I were caring for a new child. I was in the process of going from being one of the top subprime loan officers in the country and living in a 3,500 sq. ft. estate I had worked my butt off for, to foreclosing on our home and being reduced to almost nothing. Those were some dark days as I struggled mightily to pick up the pieces of what little I had left so that I could start over.

As I was getting ready to start my goal of making 200 calls for the day, I heard a "beep, beep, beep" and sprang up to investigate. It was the sound of a tow truck backing into my driveway. I knew instantly that the driver was there to take our car, which didn't register at first because the bankruptcy court had permitted us to keep one car. That car!

As I headed out the door to stop it, I yelled to my wife, "You didn't make the payment? We can't miss a payment on *that* car! What were you thinking?"

In my mind, I was thinking, "She knew better! She knew we had to keep the lease current on that car," before turning my full attention to the tow truck driver.

I soon learned that when you file for bankruptcy, the court may permit you to keep one car. Unfortunately, a car company will definitely take back a leased car, even if you've made all the payments on time, like I had.

I was livid. And like I often did during that time, my ego kicked in, and I defaulted to a defend-and-deflect mentality. I looked for somebody to blame and lashed out at my wife, the tow truck driver, and the car leasing company. That was quickly followed by blaming the housing market, my boss, and life in general.

It was all their fault, and I wanted all of them to pay for it as I stood in my driveway and watched the tow truck take our last car away from our young family.

So, I was reduced to getting around on a beach cruiser bike, which, as fate would have it, was stolen a few weeks later by a homeless man. That made it even more challenging for me to get to the small cubicle I had rented out several miles from our home as a base of operations to start rebuilding my life. I tell myself now that, as badly as I needed that bike at the time, I guess that thief needed it more. I had been humbled many times over, and I was beginning to sense a change in who I was and who I needed to be.

My Implode-O-Meter reached its limit that day. It was a reckoning as I walked back into the house and faced my wife, who had the most horrible look of fear on her face. It was a look I'll never forget. At that moment, I realized it wasn't her fault, the car company's fault, or the current conditions in the housing industry.

The only person to blame was me. I stopped yelling on the outside and raging on the inside. I simply sat in the silence of failure, welling up with tears. If you want the consummate definition of one man's discomfort zone, this was it.

I had to take ownership to get out of this mess, create a future for our family that we could be proud of, and gain the kind of financial freedom I'd so desperately wanted my entire life. Although I'm not proud to admit it, up until this time in my life, I can't say that I ever fully took ownership of anything. As I've learned, taking responsibility is not really the ego's thing.

Pointing the finger of blame at everyone else is so much easier than at yourself, isn't it?

I had so many reasons—honestly, they were excuses—not to live an amazing life and be proud when I looked in the mirror. Although my ego carried me through when times were good, it also failed me when times turned bad.

That moment in the driveway changed everything. It was the day I realized the most important thing that would forever change my life.

You can have reasons or results, but you can't have both.

In the days that followed, I finally accepted that I had been focusing on my reasons for failure instead of on how to get results. My ego used my reasons and built them around me like a fortress, unconsciously thinking they would protect me. The only thing it did was prevent me from driving results that would lead me to financial freedom.

Most of us don't move the needle in the areas we want to because we haven't acknowledged an issue yet. We haven't been honest with ourselves. Instead, we prefer to push the blame onto the people and circumstances around us. This is how the dark side of an unchecked ego works against us. I was guilty of this thinking and paid a heavy price for it.

My Process for Recovering from a Setback

It took some heavy blows before I came up with a system I still use to help me recover from setbacks. If you've gone through a lot like I have, you may already have a similar system in place. The key is to find something that makes sense and works well for you.

Here's what I do.

I set aside an assigned amount of time in my mind where I am allowed to grieve, yell, scream, cuss, or whatever I need to do to let the moment or setback pass. The timeframe and intensity are different but necessary depending on the situation, and your timeframe needs to be whatever length works for you. That can be a few seconds, five minutes, or a full day. The key is to box in the setback so it does not continue to linger and grow.

Sometimes, I also list as many as a hundred things I am grateful for, which flips my mindset. It isn't easy, but perseverance never is. I can't be frustrated and grateful at the same time, and neither can you. Frustration and anger, purged through gratitude, are powerful, and you will feel a world of difference when you process setbacks this way.

I also ask several questions that immediately bring down the temperature when I stop and think about the answers. Here are several I use:

What part of this is in my control?

Have I been through worse?

What can I learn from this?

Is this a dead end or redirection?

What action can I take that my future self will thank me for?

What about this opportunity can I or will I be grateful for?

Using these tactics helps me maintain a perseverance mindset so that I'm not overwhelmed or paralyzed by inaction.

2

Developing Self-Leadership

As you work on the individual parts of your discomfort zone to gain greater insights into your past, you must also start to look forward by reworking your approach to life.

Consider the story of Moses. His life was a constant battle of upheaval and change, requiring him to follow God's will and make critical decisions responsible for followers who put their trust in him and the Lord. As history reveals to us, Moses was both a humble servant and leader. Widely regarded as one of the most important prophets in Judaism, Christianity, and Islam, Moses was also a noted Biblical figure with many accomplishments that were a direct result of his leadership and ability to persevere through challenges.

According to the book of Exodus, God revealed himself in a burning bush and called on Moses to deliver 600,000 enslaved and persecuted Israelites from Egypt. The Pharaoh Ramses II reluctantly granted their release after a series of plagues decimated Egypt, but then sent his army after them. God parted the Red Sea for the Israelites to pass, but drowned the Egyptians who were close behind. After Moses received the Ten Commandments at Mount Sinai, he and the Israelites wandered the desert for 40 years as punishment for their lack of faith and disobedience to God. Their time in the desert humbled them, and over time, they learned to rely on Him fully.

Moses' story teaches us that perseverance and faith are especially important when faced with seemingly impossible odds. Standing up as a leader for what is right isn't easy, and it can take years before the final chapter of a story reveals itself. But this is what a great leader does.

Moses' story inspires me because it reminds me a lot of my struggles. After dealing with mountains of turmoil for years, I found answers by embracing perseverance more fully as an essential part of my life and faith.

Your answers to why you want to change and how you'll accomplish that are different from mine. Part of the hard work of self-discovery is figuring out what those things are and using them to lead yourself to a better future.

Through acceptance and self-analysis, you set the stage for a deeper dive into the second principle of perseverance that will guide you through your journey.

That principle is self-leadership.

The Balance of Accountability

After the tow truck incident, I carried my reasons vs. results mentality forward and developed a Balance of Accountability.

Imagine an old-fashioned balancing scale, much like the Scales of Justice. One side of the scale is weighted with your Reasons. The other side is weighted with Results. If you're a highly functioning person who has overcome your discomfort zone, your scale will weigh heavily on the Results and less on the Reasons side.

However, for most people, it's the opposite. For accountability to work effectively, your reasons can never outweigh your results. When the reasons weigh more heavily, you cannot get the results to tip in your favor. Excuses weigh a ton, and you must gradually remove them if you want the scale to tip in your favor.

As I learned that day in the driveway, practicing self-accountability is the quickest way to do this. Accountability is the enemy of ego, and if you want the next level of achievement in your life, the weight of the results you put on your scale can quickly outweigh your reasons if you're honest or have been humbled.

Here's one way I put that thinking to work.

I've never had six-pack abs in my life, but when I started working out with a trainer, that's where she told me we could take my body, even though I was massively overweight at the time. "I've never had a six-pack, even in high school," I told her. "I don't even know if there are muscles under there to make a six-pack."

One excuse after another and a complete lack of accountability.

But then I started shifting my scale off the reasons and onto the results by surrendering to the process. What if I worked out for an hour and a half five times a week? Or focused on nutrition and portion control? When I made these changes and a few others, I literally and figuratively started to tip the scale in my favor. Focused on driving results, and over the next year, I lost 75 pounds. My six-pack abs were still to come, but at least I knew they were there.

The same thing happens in our work. I can't count the times I've heard, "I can't sell today because I have to smooth out the paperwork with the processor," or, "I can't prospect today because I'm fixing XYZ problems."

Being busy is not the same as being productive. Being busy emphasizes reasons. Being productive emphasizes results. But we tend to stay in the busy zone because it makes us feel important. We check things off imperfect to-do lists that feed our ego, much like getting dopamine hits when a social media post goes viral. It feels good, but when you're stuck in the busy zone, the results are meaningless because those things rob you of your initiative instead of contributing to the results you want.

That day in the driveway was a gift to me because, for the first time, I realized that my reasons for not achieving financial freedom could never be the weight on my scales again. I started the commitment to adjusting the Balance of Accountability on my scale, and it started changing my life.

It became less of a battle of being bogged down in perseverance and more about creating positive momentum that allowed me to scale up my life in ways I couldn't fully imagine.

Where Self-Leadership Starts

When you live in a discomfort zone, the first thing you must do is acknowledge you have limiting beliefs. I've already mentioned your ego's role in shielding you from your shortcomings, so you must first win that battle before moving forward.

Deep down, you already know many things that inhabit various parts of your discomfort zone. For example, you know you're fat because you overeat and don't move enough. You know you don't make as much money as possible because you don't consistently work hard enough at the right things. Your relationships may be problematic because you're putting yourself first or have unreasonable expectations from others.

Until now, they've probably felt more like annoyances instead of giant boulders standing in the way of where you want to go. You've tolerated being weighed down by these heavy anchors that hinder progress, thinking you'll try to correct them one day, or better yet, they'll simply fade away with time.

If so, how's that working out for you?

Developing self-leadership requires a lot more work than simply destroying your discomfort zones. Much like creating a strategic business plan, you must also build and activate a plan to move past persistent perseverance and directly deal with the things causing you the most pain.

Generating momentum is a simple process to create. The key is how dedicated you are to removing barriers and limiting beliefs. Remember, you're fighting against years of learned and inherited poor habits that have held you back.

Instant Implementation

The key to massive momentum is instant implementation. Procrastinating makes no sense due to the fear of failure or lack of time. You must lead yourself through limiting beliefs to create your best possible outcomes as quickly as you can. Understand that you only truly fail when you lack the implementation of something you desire. The worst outcome of inaction is that you'll learn nothing new and become more frustrated by your lack of common sense and courage to make your life better.

The Challenge of Letting Go

Rooting out deeply embedded habits and ways of thinking isn't easy. By its nature, your brain is wired to gravitate to what it knows, even if what it knows isn't best for you and your future self. We also adopt habits others create because we trust them or want to be liked. That doesn't mean they are in *our* best interests.

To move forward, you must be honest with yourself. Set your ego aside. Don't blame others. Instead, hold yourself accountable. Again, this will be hard to do, but there is no other way around it. The goal is to let go of the things hurting or holding you back. Letting go also means believing you can persevere through new and unknown challenges.

It's also important to understand that your personal and professional lives are intertwined, and changing one usually affects the other. Fix one, and by default, you'll usually improve the other.

Letting go often starts with a nagging feeling. You can't put your finger on it. You just know you're capable of more and can function at a higher and happier level. This feeling may build for years until you reach a moment of clarity. Then, for no apparent reason, you have an "a-ha" thought strike you like a bolt of lightning. You may not fully realize that this lightning strike isn't spontaneous. It's been building in you for years until it finally bursts into the solution you so desperately want.

I've had many "a-ha" thoughts, but two in my business life best illustrate the point.

When I started in the mortgage industry in my twenties, I quickly worked my way into management and was making a good salary of about $100,000 annually. But I was bothered by the fact that I thought I could do better as a loan officer who could generate commissions far above that amount. The gamble was that I would give up my management job and the safety of a guaranteed salary to go on straight commission. If I wanted to do better financially, I had to gamble on myself. Letting go of that security wasn't easy, but in my gut, I knew I could do better.

So, I became a commission-only loan officer, which turned into one of the best moves I ever made. In less than two months, I became the top salesperson in our company, and my first commission check was $33,000. I've never looked back or regretted that decision, and I've been on commission ever since.

A few years later, when I first started my business, I was working 40 hours a week planting seeds through Internet lead marketing and another 40 hours a week building a full-service business. During the Christmas holiday, I turned off the lead-generating portion of my business, like I always do, to focus on spending more time with my family.

This particular Christmas was especially tough because my dad was stricken with pancreatitis and ended up in the ICU, where he fought for his life for three months. Because he was so sick, all my attention was focused on him. I quietly worked from his hospital room, but never turned on the lead marketing part of my business while there. I never had to turn it back on again, and I was pleasantly surprised that people were still reaching out to me. But letting go after prospecting this way for 13 years as the primary way to feed my family brought me to a moment of clarity that I didn't need to buy leads to thrive.

After I realized my business was doing quite nicely without this overlay, I also realized I had built enough of a referral-based business that I no longer needed to do that extra prospecting grind for 40 hours a week. So, I never worked that part of my business again, and with that newfound block of time, I focused on the more financially lucrative things for me.

There is one other letting go example that has had a huge impact on my life, and I still do it every day.

I have let go of many of my worldly problems and given them to God. That's not always easy because I'm often tempted to fix problems alone.

Your relationship with your faith is highly personal, as my faith is to me. I can tell you that as hard as it was at first for me to let go and change my way of thinking, the more I have leaned into my faith, the more peace it has brought me. In a moment of clarity, I let go of the idea that I was a better driver of my life by trying to grab the wheel from the strongest force in the universe. Instead, I realized that I was better riding shotgun and letting Jesus drive my faith, my peace, and my success. I pray every day to remind myself that I'm not alone in my journey and that I've got the best driver in the world guiding me to places I couldn't go on my own.

Letting go gives you the clarity to no longer accept reasons why you're not more successful. With this new way of thinking, you'll no longer accept reasons. You are now going to focus on results.

When you've reached this level of awareness, I want you to do a brain dump of everything that brings you discomfort. You're going to create a Reasons or Results chart and fill it in because that process turns something in your head into a stark reality you can't avoid when you see it on paper. The purpose is to change you from a victim mindset to a solutions mindset.

You must list the **reasons** for your discomfort and add the **results** you want. Those two elements naturally lead to the **solutions** you must add to finish the equation.

Here is a simple version of that chart. This is what the start of self-leadership looks like.

REASONS + SOLUTIONS = RESULTS		
REASONS	**SOLUTIONS**	**RESULTS**
My production is too low	Complete my activity tracker weekly	Close 20 deals per month
I'm broke	Save 20% of every check	6 months reserves in bank
I'm burnt out	Exercise and journal every day	Having fun

Ten Self-Leadership Questions to Ask Yourself

1. What is your biggest fear?

2. Are you obsessed with the possibility of going broke?

3. Do you mask pain with drugs, alcohol, or other forms of addiction?

4. Can you bounce back quickly from rejection?

5. Are you afraid of repeating the same actions that will lead to the same bad outcomes?

6. What creates anxiety, sadness, or shame in your life?

7. Do you worry too much about being judged by others in your personal life and on all the BS of social media?

8. What situations do you procrastinate in?

9. What happens if you pursue your "why"?

10. What happens if you pursue your passion?

Since fear is usually at the root of your discomfort zone, ask if it is a fear of failure or loss, letting others down, not being good enough, and losing love from those you care about, or is it something else?

Negative emotions signal that something is wrong or threatening, pushing us to cope with various situations. However, coping with those negative emotions also generates emotional pain. It can be debilitating when you don't take the needed steps to push through them.

Creating your Reasons or Results chart may take days, but that's okay. Keep a running list because once you've uploaded these things to your brain, it will continue to spit out answers until the question about what causes discomfort has been fully answered. Also, reach out to others in your business or personal networks. Get their opinions to confirm or deny what you suspect about yourself. What they think and what you believe may be two entirely different things, which in and of itself is a discomfort zone rooted in disconnection. Often, the truth is found somewhere in between.

As you look at your list, you'll have a good idea of where the most significant issues are. You can't take all of these on at once and not be depressed or overwhelmed, so the key is to prioritize the most important challenges and which ones will produce the biggest returns on your life in the least amount of time if you eliminate them. Think of it as eating an elephant one bite at a time.

The Activity Tracker

For example, let's say you want to double your income. You've wished that were the case for years, but you seem to have plateaued. I started doubling my Activity Tracker for that particular piece of my discomfort zone. It looks like this.

ACTIVITY TRACKER

Weekly Goals:				Week: 1	
Calls:	Hours Prospected:	Conversations:	Meetings:
NEW Business Meetings:	Events:	Social Posts:	Thank You Cards / Gifts:

Meetings:	Source		Source		Source		Source
	Total Client Meetings:		Total Referral Partner Meetings:		Total Meetings:		

NEW Business Meetings:

Events:

Conversations:	TTorLM	Source		TTorLM	Source		TTorLM	Source		TTorLM	Source
				Total Conversations:			Total Calls Made:				

Thank You Cards / Gifts:

			Total TY Cards / Gifts:

Double prospecting increased my income from $200k to $2 million in a few short years.

Why? Because I bought into the concept that doing more of the right things translates into more of the right results when consistency and accountability are behind it.

For example, I learned to fully understand the value of wearing a suit while holding open houses to command more presence and authoritative respect. I gained confidence in putting on events for hundreds of attendees. And, while it's tough to measure, I also slowly overcame

my fear of how I looked after battling self-image problems for many years. Now I work in the industry tat-
tooed from head to toe, focusing less on image and
more on outstanding outcomes for my clients.

What Are Your Elements of Self-Leadership?

As you work through your Balance of Accountability
and Activity Tracker, you'll soon start to spot strengths
and weaknesses that work for and against you. Because
you are turning the corner and now beginning to face
forward to your future, you must decide what values to
embrace. These overarching character traits are critical
to defining how you'll make decisions and creating the
energy that will drive your momentum. They will also
narrow your focus as you tune out all the useless noise
you encounter daily.

What are these elements? It depends. I have a
list that is meaningful to me. Your list needs to be as
important to you, though it will be much different.
Understand that this is a living list meant to be flexible as you grow and learn. Some of your elements will
change over time as you add new and more effective
elements that better serve the person you have become.
Others may drop off as you grow and find more effective elements that promote your self-leadership better.

Here are the 12 elements of self-leadership I use to
lock in momentum.

Practice Discipline

Discipline is about consistency and removing emotions that produce wild swings in productivity and outcomes. Using discipline to my advantage requires being fully present and fully immersed in my life's biggest goals.

I always try to remove impulsive thoughts and actions in favor of following through on the tasks that produce the biggest returns for where I want to go. Discipline is the most important factor in completing these tasks and actions, which is how we are all judged.

Discipline Defined

Discipline is the mastery of doing what one doesn't want to do. Small steps of discipline over time become big leaps in momentum. Sometimes, you may need a short break to reset your course, especially when you're growing and changing. But with appropriate discipline, these breaks should be short, measured, and purposeful. Discipline can be flexible within a given framework, but you must not deviate or lose sight of the big picture. Discipline is all about maintaining energy and flow, building habits so that your level of discipline becomes second nature and serves you well, instead of viewing discipline as another barrier to overcome.

The Ability to Make Decisions

Discipline is closely aligned with the ability to make decisions. Of course, I want quality in my decision-making process, but I also understand that I won't always get things right. However, being wishy-washy is worse than getting a decision wrong. When I decide and act on something, I know exactly how I'm advancing my cause. Right or wrong, I'm smarter and use the outcomes to confirm my path or adjust to set a new course of action. In fact, I learn more from my failures than I do from my successes.

Act with Assertiveness and Conviction

Great leaders inspire others with confidence and a clear path of how and when to execute plans and ideas. Self-leadership is much the same, except I can't BS my way through my thought processes as easily as I can with others. That means, in my heart, I must sell myself on an idea and a path forward. With this mindset, I find it easy to sell myself and confirm it by asking why this may not be the right path. If I don't come up with a good answer, that's more confirmation for me.

Courage goes hand in hand with these things. I know my brain and my ego will fight me on this because being assertive is perceived as a risk, but you know what . . . I do it anyway!

Be Authentic

By this stage, I must hold true to the person I've become and who I want to be. People closest to me will know when I'm being a phony, so why bother? If so, without authenticity, I find it impossible to feel good about what I'm working to accomplish. I know what I stand for. I know what I'm against, which factors into every decision in my self-leadership equation.

Be a Good Listener

As somebody who felt invisible for much of my life, I value being a good listener when others speak to me now, although I still struggle with this. I also pay close attention to those who aren't good listeners when talking to them. It's a sign of disrespect not to give people the present moment attention they deserve. However, I do struggle with people who are driven by their egos, even if they have a lot of worthy things to say, which is ironic because I used to listen to my ego all the time.

Let Go of the Past

I've covered this quite a bit already, but I can never state this enough times. I couldn't be entirely free to explore my future until I finally let go of the worst parts of my past, and I gave my life over to God. I'm still a work in progress, but when I finally decided to make a complete and clean break from all the trauma I endured, I started to grow and see results in my life, much like a blind man whose sight had been restored for the very first time. Put another way, the rear-view mirror of your life is a lot smaller than the windshield for a reason.

Be Resilient

This book could have easily used resilience in the title. It's slightly different from perseverance and deserves a separate place in my elements of self-leadership because it speaks to the mental toughness necessary to survive and eventually thrive in the face of adversity. For me, resilience goes hand in hand with perseverance, but I'm also aware that it is vital in its own way. You don't just need to get up. You need to get up fast over and over again.

Practice Gratitude

I could have easily died many times over. But I'm still here, and I fully believe that's because I must still achieve a purpose in life. I'm even more grateful for my wife, Kimberly, and my daughters, Brooklyn and London. They are God's greatest gifts to me and have been my muses for turning my life around. They inspire me. They fill me with joy and love. They have always stood by me in all my battles. No matter what else life throws at me, I am grateful for them and all the other blessings I have in life. Practicing gratitude daily is the key. You can't be mad and grateful at the same time.

Self-Acceptance

For years, I felt I was my worst enemy. I didn't realize that I needed to accept my shortcomings to advance in my life, but only after I understood that I need to balance those things by also appreciating the gifts I've been given. Self-acceptance is not about seeing myself as perfect or flawed. It's about being okay with who I am while trying to take small steps every day to become a better version of myself.

Time Management

It's no secret that time is our most valuable asset, and I've learned that if I piss it away without a care in the world, I'll regret where I end up. We trade time for money way too often, without thinking fully about the consequences of how much it will cost us in terms of time. Several small chapters in my life have taught me this lesson. I've taken some hard knocks and made them worse by wasting time on projects and people who don't serve me well. In those instances, in addition to any financial costs I can usually find a way to recoup, I've paid dearly for lost days, weeks, and years that I'll never get back.

Today, I fully respect how I use my time and apply maximum discipline using strict time blocking and following a daily calendar to maximize my productivity.

Commitment to Continued Growth

Once I understood who I was at any given time versus who I ultimately wanted to be, a commitment to growth and change came quickly. As you've read, I've come a long way from my early days, and while I'm happier with who I am now, I know that my happiness still depends on continuing to steer directly into my truths and the things I'm passionate about. I've also found that when I do this, I'm not working because I'm enjoying the journey as I discover new truths every day.

Self-acceptance and reflection make this possible. That awareness forces me to remain vigilant about what I've done and what I want to do going forward. Self-reflection is also about being honest and using what I find as a tool to measure and monitor how I want to grow. This is closely aligned with my final self-leadership element . . . spiritual health.

Spiritual Health

I can't stress enough how much God has helped me heal and find peace. More than that, living for Jesus has also significantly improved my relationships and focused my moral compass on the things worth fighting for, starting with Him, then my wife and children, and radiating outward to all my other relationships. This has been much more fulfilling than living for myself like I did in the past.

Once I developed a relationship with God and significantly improved my spiritual health, I became more energized, focused, and purposeful in how I wanted to live my life. I learned a valuable lesson that you must have something bigger than yourself that drives you.

■ ■ ■

Armed with the Balance of Accountability, my Reasons and Results, doubling down on actions that directly contribute to my success, and a clear understanding of self-leadership elements to guide me, I'm as prepared as possible to tackle my mental challenges.

Self-leadership is a process for all of us. You don't simply flip a switch and turn on what you need to overcome your challenges. Self-leadership is a living and flexible approach that prepares you to fight battles after putting yourself in the best possible frame of mind.

When you apply these tools to your unique situation, you've taken important steps to strengthen your emotional toughness. At the same time, you persevere in overcoming your mental challenges as well.

If you can implement these practices, you've come a long way, but understand that some of the hardest parts of persevering are still to come.

3

Putting Plans into Practice

Until now, you've been building a mental framework, fighting battles to overcome your past.

You've started the process of positively working on yourself by developing a critical self-leadership mental mindset and building a foundation that you'll continue to refine as you go forward. You have weathered setbacks and challenges, creating mental perseverance and equipping you to move forward.

Perhaps you have started putting some of these things to work for you. But now, you need to transform your new ways of thinking, understanding, and acceptance into action.

You may think you're done with perseverance, but the fact remains, you still need perseverance more than ever. It's just that you need perseverance of a different kind.

Enduring poor thinking and situations you thought were beyond your control is part of creating your perseverance mindset. It forces you to think honestly about what you can and cannot control.

That's a nice start, but it's not enough.

You must take what you've learned about yourself and turn that knowledge into actionable habits.

Create Success Habits and Routines

When you strip away the negativity that doesn't serve you well, you're left with a blank canvas representing the new life you want to create.

That leads to an important question everyone must answer.

Where and how do I get started?

Armed with discipline and a list of the elements of self-leadership unique to you, you are much better equipped to overcome doubt and self-criticism and replace them with confidence and self-esteem.

After years of thinking and refining how I wanted to move forward with my life, I discovered what serves me better than all the others.

Habits and routines.

These elements of consistency are what make hundreds and thousands of small victories possible. Those small victories compound over time. Creating structure down to the smallest details makes the larger wins possible.

For example, I used to wake in the morning, smoke a cigarette, drink a bunch of coffee to help get rid of a hangover, eat donuts, and immediately start checking my email by 6:30 a.m. every morning.

But here is the routine I now follow every morning.

I wake up at 4:45 a.m., while the world is still quiet, and I can go through my mental preparation for the day. I place a high value on controlling this part of my day. It brings me peace and clarity on several levels.

A typical morning for me looks like this.

Pray, practice gratitude, read devotionals, and other materials.

Write a journal entry and text it to my VIPs.

Do a 20-minute Peloton session and a 60-minute session with my trainer.

Take a red light sauna

Take a cold plunge while meditating and reading affirmations because what we say to ourselves matters.

Only then do I get ready for work.

After I go through this self-care routine, I make a cup of coffee for my wife and take my daughter to school when I can or somehow connect with her, often by making breakfast sandwiches, which are my specialty. I also make time to spend with my dogs, which never fails to lift my spirits.

I view these important rituals as making deposits for myself before others can make withdrawals.

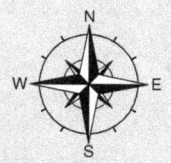

Protecting Your Mind

Protecting your mind and what you feed it is as important as anything you do each day. If you program your brain with negativity from outside influences, you won't be surprised when that's what you unintentionally push out to the world. Be careful about what you decide to absorb every day because what you choose to let in defines you on the inside and what the world sees from you on the outside.

If you don't like the current version of you, change your environment, what you consume, and the people you associate with. These things, more than any others, have the most significant influence on your reaching your full potential.

I *do not* check business emails or business text messages until it's "go" time. Part of the reason for this is that I've already printed out my daily calendar the night before, and I'm already aware of my obligations for the current day. When I turn my attention to business, I review that calendar again and visualize the outcomes I want, problem-solving at all hours of the day.

I'm always prospecting in one form or another. Retaining existing clients or acquiring new clients is a top priority, whether I'm working from home, in the office, or on the road.

There are also days when I invest in myself and my team with an ongoing commitment to seminars, classes, and continuing education. That growth is vital on an individual and an organizational level.

I can accomplish these things because time management is critical for me. If it doesn't add to my day, I do whatever I can to eliminate or delegate it. I fully buy into the idea that saying "yes" to something means saying "no" to something else, so I'm constantly weighing my options and decisions carefully. It's a constant battle because I'm naturally inclined to be a "yes" man.

My approach to time management helps me accomplish a lot in the most efficient way possible. But I'm also aware that balance is essential for a healthy outlook on life, so there are days I designate as "prep" days or "play" days to complement "power" days, forming what I like to call the Three Ps of time management, which I'll dive into deeper later in this book.

Transform Routines into Revenue

It's not enough to create routines you think will serve you well. The key is leveraging them in ways that put money in your pocket in the most effective way possible.

Early in my career, one of the things I did while working in our company call center was being strategic when I placed calls and followed up with potential clients. Instead of a shotgun approach that meant calling at all hours, I arranged my call obligations by time zone. I had figured out that some parts of the day were better than others for reaching people.

For example, if you're in California and want to make calls to Virginia or New York, don't call at 3 p.m. west coast time because that's in the heart of the dinner hour for families on the east coast. Think about it. How often have you welcomed a call during your dinner hour when your primary focus is spending time with your family? By calling at noon, 5 p.m., or after 7 p.m., I had a much higher success rate at reaching people who were more ready and willing to discuss business.

In business, you compete with many things, but the last group of people you want to compete with when reaching out to a prospect is that person's family. Showing respect that way also put me in a better position than others in the mortgage industry who didn't respect these boundaries. It was a simple routine, but it opened a lot of doors for me and drove my success.

The other routine I developed that was also effective and lucrative was working on things "closest to the wallet."

If you're unfamiliar with that term, "closest to the wallet" is exactly what it sounds like. I prioritized actions on deals in the nearest timeframe to pay me for my work. In the mortgage business, you have loans that are funded in a "today" timeframe, and those are the deals where I concentrated my efforts first. Much like you don't want to put together a game-winning drive in a football game and march 99 yards downfield only to be stopped on the 1-yard line, my approach put every effort into carrying that ball over the goal line for a score.

With "today" items handled, I turned my attention to ensuring documents out for closings were correctly executed, ensuring they were either signed or locked in for a time and place to be signed with all parties present. Following this priority chain, I then made sure that documents for approved loan funding in the near future were being pulled and in order.

With these "closest to the wallet" deals in order, I turned my attention to new loans and files in various stages of submission, using that time to push other deals closer to funding.

After all of my existing client files were in order, I focused the balance of my time on prospecting to ensure the other parts of the "closest to the wallet" activities remained as part of a full pipeline. Because I prioritized time management and efficiency, I was often done with existing files by noon many days, leaving me 6–8 hours for labor-intensive prospecting activities. Using my time zone approach was also an optimal use of my time.

The Open House Strategies

Structuring my in-office work days this way has put a lot of money in my pocket over the years. But in the mortgage business, not every day is an in-office day. On weekends, the industry's focus is centered on open houses. As loan officers, we're expected to join Realtors on-site. They often suggest joining them, typically from noon to 4 p.m. on a Saturday or Sunday, to greet potential buyers. That's a common practice, but that doesn't mean it's the best practice, which I quickly figured out.

When I was asked to house sit with various Realtors during a four-hour block, I would counter by asking if I could come by from 2 to 4 p.m. instead and hang out afterward to help clean up signs and debrief. Realtors were always happy with this arrangement, which was good news for me because I used that noon to 2 p.m. block to hit up 10 other open houses where I would meet other Realtors. I was still able to spend quality time with my primary Realtor and capture all the leads from their open house at the end of it, but I was also able to plant 10 additional seeds of new business.

At other times, I would bring my daughters with me to open houses. After entering a home, I'd introduce myself but not let the Realtor know I was a loan officer. My girls and I would walk around the house casually, sending the unspoken message that I was a family man and letting them make a first impression before we spoke.

After our house tour, I'd reintroduce myself and let the Realtor know I was a loan officer, but what made me different is that I had a list of a hundred pre-approved loan clients actively looking for a home. Then, I'd explain how I was looking for my agent partners and ask them if their current lender does this for them. I knew the answer was "no" because nobody was doing it then. Agents were always blown away at this stranger who walked through the door just a few minutes earlier and was ready to help them sell a home.

In addition to this valuable list, I told them I had an open house kit I was dropping off to my partners, but I had an extra one for them. Then I would go out to my car and grab one of the kits prepared that included snacks, water, and a packet of information as a leave-behind item for them. It was a nice touch that demonstrated I had taken great care to start a business relationship with them and that I valued their business. But the fortune is in the follow up, which I was very good at.

As you can imagine, not only did I plant seeds for success by routinely doing this, but I also built a vast network and created a lot of opportunities to grow and do well financially. The other big benefit of working this way was spending quality time with my girls while instilling my work ethic in them. Not surprisingly, they both now want to be in the real estate industry.

How can you replicate these success routines for your line of work? Thinking above and beyond and outside the box applies to all types of sales situations, but can also apply to all parts of your life. Cooking your spouse's favorite meal "just because" or taking your team out for drinks and dinner are great ways to show you value people who are essential in your life. Getting into the success routine of doing small acts like this can have long-lasting positive impacts that will show you care and build successful relationships that pay off in several ways over a lifetime.

Refine Your Resilience Roadmap

Overcoming hard things can have you looking over your shoulder. Feeling insecure is normal when you first try new things. Many people give up too early and never fully realize their business and personal potential.

They are always waiting for the next shoe to drop instead of understanding that shoes will always drop, and it's up to them to figure out the best ways to pick them up! What some people haven't learned yet is that doing hard things builds self-confidence.

When you avoid doing hard things, you slowly erode it.

Resilience is the companion of perseverance. They are similar but distinct, as we've discussed.

What makes them so important is that resilience and perseverance are all about understanding the biggest shadow self you have inside of you.

Fear.

There are several ways to cope with fear. You may not fully overcome it, which is a tall task. For me, the best thing I can hope for is to manage my fears effectively. It places less pressure on me when I accept fear as part of the process, knowing that I own it instead of it owning me.

 ### Fear Is the Enemy of Progress

When we feed into fear, it can paralyze us. Our anxiety rises, and our brain protects us by shutting down against what is interpreted as a threat. A more natural and relaxed state is one of faith.

We're built for faith; calling on it to help us lean into our fears is a powerful ally. Faith and perseverance give us the confidence to push through our challenges to the other side and win.

The most effective tool I use in fighting fear is faith.

Faith over fear is the bridge we need in times of doubt. It can carry us anywhere we want to go. You get to map out that journey by choosing how you put your faith in God, others, and yourself.

Faith is the unseen belief that you are worthy and can do what seems impossible. We become mighty when we lean into faith, pushing aside the fear. Faith reinforces the idea that we can and deserve to win. It helps us overcome fear, which is the enemy of our dreams.

Faith also makes resilience possible. Practicing resilience means getting back up after getting knocked down, and this ability to rebound is just as important as the first step we take on whatever journey we're on. Our habits and routines are rooted in discipline, but resilience carries us across the finish line. Resilience is a mental toughness mindset that can take us to any destination we choose.

If you're not sold on the concepts of faith and resilience, simply ask yourself if you would rather go through life with an "I'm not sure it can be done" mindset instead. The answer should be obvious to you. If not, you've still got a lot of self-leadership work to do.

I think it's curious that so many of us have already overcome so many challenges in our lives, yet we question whether we can overcome the simplest ones of today. Remember all you have already accomplished and persevered to this point, and allow that to be a catalyst through whatever challenges you have in your life now.

As you become more familiar with how to effectively fight fear, each battle becomes less of a confrontation until fear loses its power over us. Stacking wins through action slowly wipes out that paralyzing grip, and instead of taking flight from what we fear as a first response, we turn into fighters because we're focused and have the tools we need to get the results we want.

Quiet the Noise

Overcoming fear requires quieting the noise of all that is unimportant from the past and eliminating thoughts of a future that no longer exists. That harmful noise creates unnecessary disruption in your present day, distracting you from the focus you seek.

Know where your fear comes from and shut it down by regrouping to the present moment and who you are now, combining it with gratitude and appreciation for the day and moment you are in.

Completely rewiring how you think and turning your thoughts into actions isn't an easy or neat process. You must still confront your demons and shortcomings daily to create the best possible outcome. Understand that they will always be a part of who you are, but that you are now in control because you have focused your efforts on important goals and processes that will now rule your life for years.

You don't always need to fight with your fears. Acceptance and acknowledgment are often better ways to accomplish this. Frequently, the best outcomes for these kinds of fights happen when you simply drop the gloves so you can actively turn your attention to things that matter more in your life.

4

Tapping into a Support System

If you want to experience the most challenging form of perseverance, try surrounding yourself with the wrong team.

Ask anyone who has ever achieved anything worthy, and they will tell you the people backing, supporting, mentoring, and guiding them to greatness played a huge role in their success. Nobody excels in a complete vacuum.

Several people have helped me on my path to success, but none has been more important than my wife, Kimberly. She was a rock of support as I started and grew my business, helping me get through some dark days while anchoring our home life as a great mother to our girls. We've also grown and enjoyed success together in business. Since she transitioned to a more active role in our business ventures, Kimberly has also become one of the most successful rainmakers I know.

Often, we only see the face of success, like Kobe Bryant on a basketball court or Elon Musk in a boardroom. But they're the tip of the iceberg, the 10% we see, not the 90% below the surface. Yet, none of these people, or anyone in a leadership position, could accomplish much without the contributions of those supporting them.

The same holds true in your life. You have coworkers, mentors, coaches, friends, and family who are there for you. They have your best interests at heart and know that your success is reflected on them in a shared success.

High achievers focused on winning know that great teams take time to build, but if done correctly, they consistently lead to more wins. Leaders of these teams have complete awareness that winning is a team sport. They also appreciate that although you may have some superstars in your organization, others who fill vital roles are just as important to the team's overall success.

Great leaders must be in the moment as much as possible. They must continuously gauge talent and find ways to blend individual talents and skills to create a cohesive support system that functions optimally and rewards everyone on the team.

 **Collaboration Is Magic**

Giving others what they truly need is how to make the best version of that magic. It is even more special when you receive what you need in return, which is usually the case. As a leader, your collaborative contributions can range from encouragement and leadership to practical tools and removing barriers. And you must do this in a way that shows everyone's input is encouraged and welcome. The results are often outsized and unexpected, making collaboration an exciting and dynamic tool you should master in all situations.

It has been said that learning to build a great team and tap into it effectively is perhaps the most difficult skill for leaders to learn. A leader must have patience and perseverance, understand the nature of trial and error, and be a great judge of talent. They must also closely listen to input, weed out distractions, apply critical analysis, and adjust each participant's roles and contributions as quickly as possible. One of the most important elements is mutual trust, which is based on clear communication and shared goals.

Using these metrics and others, a leader must know how to build teams and utilize their networks based on a deep understanding of how interlocking talents and skills will best meet the challenges.

It's not easy against rapidly changing conditions, especially in most business sectors, where speed is essential to winning battles. It is especially critical in a down market or challenging business periods when stress and uncertainty can complicate efforts. Those times either propel or paralyze you.

A lot of things go into building an organization that consistently wins. However, it's easy to claim that the quality of your personal and professional relationships determines the quality and quantity of your successes. You must protect the secret sauce of your relationships and of your business's culture.

Iron Sharpens Iron

"As iron sharpens iron, so one person sharpens another."
Proverbs 27:17

Do you clearly understand the types of people you need to surround yourself in your personal and professional life? This is a difficult conversation to have with yourself. Often, it means paring back or eliminating relationships that have run their course and no longer serve you well. People struggle with this because we have been taught to be kind and considerate to a fault. But you should constantly reevaluate your relationships and put total effort into mutually beneficial, positive ones that feed into your growth.

This is not a new concept. Iron sharpening iron and man's quest for improvement have been central ideas of humanity since the dawn of civilization. It sprang forth at a time when blacksmiths used a series of heating and cooling cycles to strengthen and purify iron. A single hammer blow on a raw piece of iron made little difference. Still, the blacksmith's perseverance and precision slowly created something functional and occasionally beautiful out of the iron.

In this same way, you must engage with people who challenge you. Think of exchanging ideas as a mental mindset version of iron sharpening iron. This transference amounts to your learning or using the other person's skills to sharpen your own.

Let me give you a great example of how iron sharpening iron worked in my life at a time when I desperately wanted to pursue a better way to live.

The Breakthrough

Early in my career, Jessica was a call center colleague, and we became friends over time. We sat next to each other for years, made cold calls, and grinded it out daily. We hustled and competed in our profession. We propped each other up when things weren't going particularly well, and we celebrated each other's victories when they happened.

She knew I was struggling financially, and on a break one day, she told me, "You've got to come to this coaching event. It will change your life."

Normally, I'd be all in. But from my perspective, I was on the heels of bankruptcy, making enough to cover basic needs like food, clothing, and shelter, with just a little bit left over, so urging me to go to this event was a problem for a couple of reasons. First, I didn't have the $2,500 admission fee, nor did I meet the pre-qualification of making $200,000 annually to attend.

I thanked Jessica but told her I'd have to pass. I thought I had missed out, but instead, Jessica reached into her bag, pulled out a stack of CDs, and told me, "Listen to these instead." They were filled with a ton of practical business and sales strategies, from getting warm referrals to how to build an effective team, among many others.

I was desperate and hungry to find a way to make more money, so I listened to every CD and followed exactly what they said to do. Jessica also turned me on to a seminar that only cost $500, and between both of those investments in myself, over the next 12 months, I went from making $74,000 to more than $280,000. I doubled down on the lessons I learned from the CDs, referring to them often while building on the most lucrative activities I learned and putting them into practice.

That made me hungry for more. If I could grow my income from listening to CDs, what could I do if I went all in on finding a mentor to help me reach an even higher level?

I was sold, and I wanted to step up a big way. Now, I just needed to convince my wife that I wanted to spend $2,500 per month on coaching when we had just started getting to a better spot financially. I had no clue if I could sell her that it was a good idea or not. But I knew that if I had the kind of accountability they wanted me to have, bolstered by the somewhat daunting prospect of shelling out $2,500 per month, I would win and win big.

When Kimberly agreed to let me spend that amount of money each month, I was excited, but simultaneously, the pressure on me doubled. It had to work if I were to take that kind of money away from our budget every month, which was the equivalent of our house payment at the time.

When my first coach, Josh Sigman, told me to make 100 calls, I made 200. Everything he said to do, I did double. I determined not to back down or let anyone outwork me.

What happened next exceeded all my expectations. In 36 months, my income grew from $280,000 to

$1.6 million in commissions. It was life-changing, not only in how my income grew but because it permanently changed my mindset, allowing me to see that all things are possible through perseverance.

Through this program, I learned a valuable perseverance principle.

Your future self is shaped by those who lead you today.

In my case, thanks to Jessica, who led me to my first round of success, and working with a coaching mentor, I began to create the future I'd always dreamed about.

This was a hard lesson for me to learn when I felt I was alone all my life. Although I was okay at talking to people on the phone, I didn't fully develop close relationships with people I could trust until I was well into adulthood.

My parents were never in a position to help me financially, even if they wanted to. They had their struggles with money, including helping my brothers, who lived with my parents until they were grown men in their forties.

When I was tossed out of the house at 18, I made up my mind that I would never ask for help. I thought, "I'm on my own. I need to make it happen for myself."

I was defiant and alone and felt strongly that I had to prove myself by stepping out into the world.

Until the day Jessica handed me those CDs, I had never taken much direction from anyone. I drifted, and that was leading me down a path to failure. I was a team of one, and as I've already said, you can't win with that kind of thinking.

Jessica's help at a time when my options were limited changed everything, and I owe her a huge debt of gratitude. Between her kindness and support and my coach's intense efforts to teach me about accountability, I've completely changed my thinking. Now, I'm constantly looking for the next person who can lead me to my next success in life, my marriage, finances, and my physical and mental health.

Today, you can't convince me not to find support.

Your Mentorship Matrix

We've heard it before: "You are the sum of the five people you spend the most time with." It's a powerful statement because it emphasizes our closest relationships' profound impact on our beliefs, habits, and mindset.

If that's true, and I believe it is, then let me take it further. What if, instead of solely focusing on the people who currently surround you, you actively seek out individuals who represent excellence in the most crucial areas of your life?

What would happen if you seek mentors in five key areas of your life: spiritual, financial, relationships, personal development, and work? What if you look for five people already where you want to be? Approached the right way, many successful people are generous with their time to people serious about improving their lives.

Do not be intimidated by asking these people for help. Instead, think of them as your Personal Board of Directors who can help guide you toward your highest potential. Think of them less as "yes" men and women and more as those willing to tell you "no" and the hard truths you need to hear.

For example, if marriage is your most important relationship, how would your life change if you actively seek out advice and spend time with others who have strong and happy marital relationships? Or if you're making a million dollars a year but want to grow in that area, who can you follow or approach for help who has tens of millions or even billions of dollars? If you approach life similarly in the five areas I noted, you create your Mentorship Matrix.

What would your future life look like if you did this? How would your marriage, your business, your fitness, or whatever it is you care most about change in 6 months, 1 year, 10 years?

Remember, iron sharpens iron, so you need to find the most challenging and positive relationships and continually build them. Look for people who can help carry you up the mountain. Surround yourself with the right support system by boldly seeking those further along the path you wish to walk. Their influence can help you to push through barriers, unlock new opportunities, and achieve a level of success and happiness you may have only dreamed about.

You can't do it alone, but in many people's minds, that's the great lie we're taught to believe. The truth is that it's not your performance alone that will take you to the next level—it's the systems and the people you surround yourself with to create the accountability you need to succeed.

Accountability is everything. It can be measured in big ways or small ways. For example, we had an accountability system in my coaching group. You were subject to paying a fine for everything you said you would do within a specific timeframe and didn't do. Sometimes the fines were only $50, but they were often larger.

The fines were donated to charity, so at least there was accountability and a good purpose behind it. Still, that adds up quickly when you fall short 20 or 30 times, which was the case for some of our members, including me.

When your support system and mentors build in accountability to measure your progress, it forces you to take all excuses off the table and work the system.

The time has come to ask yourself who is leading you now. Who are you learning from, whose systems are you following, and who is holding you accountable for reaching your goals? If you don't have a clear answer to these questions, assessing your situation immediately is crucial.

If you realize you are relying entirely on yourself, it's time to change immediately.

Self-reliance is important, but trying to do everything alone has its limitations. The path to success is paved with challenges that are easier to navigate when you have guidance from others who have been there before.

How Brian Chesky Designed the Ultimate Bed-and-Breakfast Business

The business world thrives on networking and building highly effective teams. It's easy to see how collaboration can produce massive results across all sectors of the economy. Trying to make the point that a support system is the difference between failure and success is easy because it is a tried-and-true formula.

Take Brian Chesky, for example. He embodies the notion of starting with nothing, using his skill set and contacts to launch an idea, and eventually building it into a household name.

In this case, that name is Airbnb.

From humble beginnings in 2007, Airbnb has grown into a community of more than 4 million hosts who have welcomed more than 1.5 billion guests in 220+ regions and countries worldwide. Chesky is also now worth close to $8 billion.

He is not a tech guy or a real estate developer. Not even close. Chesky is an industrial engineering graduate of the Rhode Island School of Design (RISD), which makes his story more interesting because he had to rely on an even more diverse network to find success. From the start, Chesky infused his design sensibility and combined it with his creative pedigree into Airbnb's culture and community.

After graduating from RISD, Chesky moved to the west coast to work as an industrial engineer, eventually settling in San Francisco to live with his classmate Joe Gebbia. The pair didn't have enough to pay their rent, so they opened their house to short-term renters as a bed-and-breakfast during the Industrial Designers Society of America Conference, when hotel rooms were impossible to find. Their first guests slept on air mattresses in their loft and dined on Pop-Tarts. They also marketed the concept to potential guests as an "air bed-and-breakfast," marking the humble birth of Airbnb.

The concept didn't catch on initially, but they believed in the commercial potential and turned to another RISD roommate, Nathan Blecharczyk, to help them. After tinkering with various business models, they settled on a final concept and began shopping Airbnb to angel investors.

They needed a hefty dose of perseverance because the first 15 investors rejected or ignored their proposals. Eventually, they connected with computer programmer and investor Paul Graham. Graham gave them $20,000 in funding and invited them to sharpen their business execution as part of Graham's collaborative startup incubator, Y Combinator. After a few more false starts, Airbnb officially launched in March 2009.

From the beginning, employees have been treated as valuable assets, working closely with host communities for a more seamless and responsive experience. For Chesky and Gebbia, earning employees' trust was as important as asking hosts to open their homes to strangers. By design, every move was collaborative in nature.

In 2011, four short years after Chesky and Gebbia inflated mattresses in their loft, Airbnb had established a presence in almost 90 countries and passed 1 million nights booked. That attracted attention from the biggest names in Silicon Valley, who invested $112 million, increasing the company's value to over $1 billion.

Although Chesky and Airbnb have become wildly successful, as a tech outlier focused on building high-functioning solutions with an engineer's logic, he had to tap into a vast network of experts who could help him scale Airbnb's rapid ascent. His reliance on a support system and community building has been Chesky's core mantra from the start.

That collaborative approach and Chesky's perseverance created one of the most noteworthy rags-to-riches stories in recent years.

Building Your Personal Board of Directors

I've already talked about optimizing the five key areas of your life. The quality of your spirituality, finances, relationships, personal development, and work defines the quality of your life. Finding mentors in each of these areas is crucial to your success. Mentors are essential, but you must also consider four other groups of people who can help you succeed.

Along with your mentors and coaches, you must look for opportunities to grow through team building, formal and informal networking, professional development, and family and friends. The five key areas of your life are uniquely intertwined with the five most important groups, creating a Personal Board of Directors to help you succeed in all your personal and professional ventures.

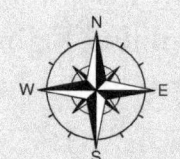 **Be Careful Who You Surround Yourself With**

Look carefully at who you are surrounded by and the activities they represent. Do this without judgment, for we have all had moments of lapsed judgment and have not been who we desire. But going forward, we must decide who we want to be and, in turn, surround ourselves with like-minded people. Not just stand with them but actively seek their counsel and offer ours to sharpen each other's iron. This is not to abandon those who are not aligned, but to offer arm's length love in a better way than it was to us.

When building your board, one of the first things to understand is that some situations are transactional-based vs. relationship-based. Relationships are more permanent and ongoing, whereas transactional relationships center around a specific action. Transactional activities have a higher attrition rate because you come together to do a deal, work through the deal, and when the deal is over, you move on.

Transactional activities are also more expensive because you're always prospecting, which takes time and money. Conducting business this way also feels like you are pricing and buying a perishable commodity, which is less than ideal. In a job setting, if you don't build strong work relationships in your company, you have a significant outlay devoted to hiring, training, rehiring, and retraining as people move on. This is why building solid relationships is beneficial in all cases.

You can also apply that same type of thinking to your personal life. It's not difficult to buy into the fact that your life is much better when you have strong core relationships instead of shuffling people in and out of your life.

Another thing to note is that not everyone around you will be able to support your growth. Change is hard and not encouraged by most; in fact, it scares most who enter it. When you change, others may feel insecure about that. Ignore their fear and know it is not your own. Stay your course of truth toward the direction you are rising. Let no one hold you back to their standard while you create your own.

When you lay a long-term foundation and put the right person in the right place, you maximize efficiency. Suppose you're a $100 per hour employee, the last thing you want to do is work that a $20 per hour employee should be doing. But that happens if you can't keep that entry-level employee happy. Much like you, they want to be a part of something where they can grow personally and contribute to a company's overall success. If they don't grow, they usually go elsewhere.

If you're a leader or an owner, most times, you'll have to step into the vacancy, undermining your momentum. Leaders also tend to feel nobody can do the job as well as they can, which may be true, and that's a trap many leaders fall into. Their lack of trust in others performing the same job at the same level is a sure way to hold business teams and entire companies back from operating at a peak level.

How many of these boxes can you fill in with people currently in your life? You don't need to fill in every box, but you should start thinking about creating an effective support system using this as a blueprint.

PERSONAL BOARD OF DIRECTORS	SPIRITUAL	FINANCIAL	RELATIONSHIPS	PERSONAL DEVELOPMENT	WORK
MENTORS					
TEAM					
NETWORKING					
PROFESSIONAL					
FAMILY & FRIENDS					

You're not starting from scratch when you build a Personal Board of Directors. Each of us already has several key support people in place. The key is to build upon what you already have. Look for multiple ways to expand your network. For instance, when you create business relationships, you're doing so with the expectation that you will create financial value through shared business deals or by extending your network, leading you to others you can do deals with.

Another benefit is that an effective Personal Board of Directors contributes to better decision-making. My board, with mentors such as Rick Ruby, Ben Newman, Rene Rodriguez, Ron Leonhardt, and others, has profoundly impacted the quality of my decisions.

Another critical element of having a Personal Board of Directors is maintaining an ongoing dialogue with them. It's rare, if at all, that you'll engage your entire board all at once, but you should reach out to all your board members at least once a quarter and when you're trying to reach a big decision or creating annual goals and standards for yourself. When in doubt, include board members in your discussions even if they don't appear to be able to help you directly. Often, a fresh set of eyes is helpful, and your board members will also have their own board members whom they can tap to advance your agenda.

Tapping into the right skill set with the right person also makes all the difference. My wife isn't as well versed in mortgage guidelines as many of my team. Still, she is a valuable business development director on my personal production team because she is an incredible networker. She can talk to anyone, and because of her positive energy, people love talking to her, too. As an effective networker, she brings clients to those on our team so they can do what they do best. Everyone wins because everyone does what they do best.

If you're a leader, one of the most effective things you can do is figure out what everyone's strengths are in your network and create situations and systems where those talents can best be used.

It's also up to you to find ways to build teams and create ways for various talents to interact with each other. I routinely hold team-building exercises, host networking events, and organize seminars, workshops, and mastermind events. One of the consequences of doing all these things is that I've met some incredible people and built relationships that have become close over time, including several people who now work directly with me on various deals.

I'm the same way in my personal life, creating opportunities for my family and friends to come together often while supporting them in ways that produce positive outcomes for things that are important to them. I also know they are there for me when I need help or just want to bounce ideas off someone I can trust.

It takes ongoing effort, but consider the outcome when you don't put in the work. Variations of the following quote have been attributed to several people, but what matters is the sentiment, which I love.

If you hang out with clowns, you'll find a circus.

Surrounding yourself with the right people means everything as you continue to grow and persevere. When things get crazy, knowing who has your back means the difference between sanity and success or unhappiness and failure.

Life is also full of surprises. You never know where a valuable contact will come from. It could be a chance meeting at an industry event, a referral from an old friend, or even a call from a seed you planted long ago. Be open, but also be selective.

Get into the habit of reaching out. Find ways to connect. Purposely seek people out who can add value to your life. Your Personal Board of Directors is the key to your success. Cultivate it like you would a garden, and soon, you'll harvest results that will pay you incredible dividends.

5

Stacking Consistent Wins

Consistency is a pure form of lasting perseverance.

You must be able to do things repeatedly over a long period, creating a worthy work standard that will move you closer to your goals in life. You cannot expect to achieve greatness in a single day, week, month, or sometimes even more extended periods, including several years.

Consistently showing up and doing the work in front of you while applying focus and wisdom requires perseverance. Consistency is the act of repeatedly grinding away, doing important tasks at hand. A perseverance mindset is the mental state you need to give you the best possible chance of not giving up or wavering, especially when an initial rush of enthusiasm dies down, and you're faced with the hard work with your goal still far from sight.

You will not succeed without consistency. There is no shortcut or substitute for it. Stacking consistent wins is not magic. It's the combination of consistently working on things you're passionate about, and some you're not, and doing them repeatedly until you succeed.

One of my favorite comedians, Jerry Seinfeld, is a model of consistency, and it's no secret he owes much of his success to sharpening his joke writing skills with a technique called "Don't Break the Chain."

From his earliest days of doing standup, Seinfeld was driven to become one of the best. He understood that to be a better comic, he had to write better jokes, and the way to create better jokes was through consistently practicing his craft every day.

He worked using a big yearlong calendar that he hung on a wall in his writing space. Every day that he wrote, he used a red magic marker and placed an X on the calendar. Those red X marks joined together to form a chain, and the goal became a game of making the chain longer every day. Although the task was writing, the goal was simplified to doing whatever it took not to break the chain.

Seinfeld understood early on that long-term consistency beats short-term intensity, which ebbs and flows daily or week to week. That approach worked out well for him, wouldn't you agree?

Consistency is what happens when our values, beliefs, and behaviors align. Consistency and perseverance are how to make sense of our place in the world. This is backed by brain science, in which our brains crave consistency and will work on our behalf to seek what is already familiar to us. Research has shown that repetitive actions form neural pathways in the brain, making these actions increasingly automatic over time. This concept, known as "neuroplasticity," suggests that consistency rewires the brain over time.

One of the reasons McDonald's sits at the top of the fast-food industry is because of its consistency. You know you're getting the same meal whenever you order a McDonald's quarter pounder with cheese. The threat of eating an unknown burger is removed, and without debating the health merits of how healthy this might be, your brain only knows the threat of bad-tasting food has been removed. Subconsciously, your brain is happy that there is no threat, and this happiness is transferred to your conscious state.

Consistency also takes many forms. For example, my focus on consistency is driven by loyalty, discipline, attention to execution, and always being driven to find solutions to the ongoing challenges of acquiring and retaining team members and clients.

External factors will continue to change, and I will react to them. But with a consistent framework in place, many decisions and stressors in my life have been removed. That allows me to focus on problems and solve them more efficiently, creating a natural momentum I can harness for better outcomes.

The Power of Momentum

Forward momentum is a series of small actions that accumulate over time. The more you gather, the more you build on them. The less you gather, the longer it takes. Remember, however, it's God's timing. Stop trying to make things happen before their time. Do your part in the small actions and leave the results to Him.

The Magic of Good Habits

Good habits are essential for effectively implementing consistency in your life. If you have bad habits and keep repeating them, you will get bad outcomes no matter how much consistency or perseverance you have.

Habits are the building blocks that lead to mastery of any skill. Many experts believe it takes as much as 10,000 hours of practice with good habits in place to master a skill. Of course, this doesn't apply to things like tying your shoe, but you must do the work if you want to become an Olympic athlete, or a titan on Wall Street, or a leader in any business endeavor.

In my business, the right habits make all the difference between success and failure, financial prosperity and average bottom lines. What do I mean by the right habits? Many loan officers think that if they put in 10,000 hours to do loans, that will be enough. That's not the case. Instead, to be an elite loan officer, they must also spend 10,000 hours successfully getting loans to become a seven-figure earner.

You will continue to evolve and grow every hour you put in the right kind of work. It may not feel like growth, but it is.

Consistency is also an important ingredient in your mental health. From the time we're children, we crave consistency in a nurturing home life. As young people, when we experience the same routines repeatedly, the brain strengthens connections that lead to trusting and secure attachments. Children who live in consistent environments also learn to regulate their emotions and behavior better because they know what to expect from the world around them.

The challenge of creating good habits over time is that our culture often rewards outcomes more than the process. It's hard to be consistent because we tend to focus on the outcome more than the process, which is backwards.

Put another way, we're more drawn to the positive feelings of outcomes rather than the struggle of the journey. Most of us quit during the struggle before we can experience the rewards of staying the course. Small positive outcomes are fine, but when we rethink how we approach things, we understand we can also enjoy dopamine hits that confirm we're on the right track instead of only thinking we'll get dopamine hits when we complete challenges.

I've learned over the years that doing the right things consistently doesn't always produce visible results, or as quickly as we want. But I'm also smart enough to know that when it comes to my mental health, affirmations, workouts, cold plunges, meditation, and other similar habits practiced consistently, it gives me the mental focus and positivity I need to be successful. I've also learned that when I take care of myself first, I'm in a good place to help others live their best lives too.

One of my favorite books on consistency is James Clear's *Atomic Habits*, a runaway bestseller for some time now. It is filled with gems about consistency, and one passage in particular about creating a new habit is well worth repeating here.

Clear starts with the premise that to create a new habit, you must make it so easy that you cannot say no. He goes on to say,

"It is easy to get bogged down trying to find the optimal plan for change: the fastest way to lose weight, the best program to build muscle, the perfect idea for a side hustle. We are so focused on figuring out the best approach that we never get around to taking action.

"When scientists analyze people who appear to have tremendous self-control, it turns out those individuals aren't all that different from those who are struggling. Instead, "disciplined" people are better at structuring their lives in a way that does not require heroic willpower and self-control.

"Over the long run, however, the real reason you fail to stick with habits is that your self-image gets in the way. This is why you can't get too attached to one version of your identity. Progress requires unlearning. Becoming the best version of yourself requires you to continuously edit your beliefs and upgrade and expand your identity."

Elements of Consistency

I'm a big fan of the Philadelphia Eagles. The team, just like the city, has a rich tradition of blue-collar, grind-it-out hard work that I admire. Over the years, I've come to appreciate the no-nonsense approach of guys like Reggie White, Fletcher Cox, and Harold Carmichael.

However, in terms of consistency, I've become a big fan of Jason Kelce in recent seasons. His brother, Travis, has gotten more attention for dating Taylor Swift and has an impressive record of accomplishments of his own. However, as an Eagles fan, Jason is my guy for several reasons.

Before he retired at the end of the 2023 season, Jason set the franchise record for 145 starts over 13 seasons, was a six-time first-team All-Pro, and a seven-time Pro Bowl attendee. As a center in the middle of massive scrums on every play, he was the other quarterback on the field. If he were off, even for one down, it could cost his team with penalties, blown blocking assignments, or a failure to move the ball down the field and score.

As an offensive lineman, his contributions were much less splashy than the team's wide receivers, running backs, or quarterback, but those who played with him knew exactly how valuable he was. They understood the team's consistent high level of play always started with Kelce's high level of play.

He was part of the team that won the Super Bowl in 2018 against the New England Patriots. Although he retired a year before the Eagles won Super Bowl LIX in the 2024 season, it was his tough-nosed approach and determination that continued to carry over to everyone on the team. Nowhere was that more apparent than with quarterback Jalen Hurts, who led the Eagles as they crushed the favored Kansas City Chiefs in a 40–22 blowout. Hurts was also named the Super Bowl MVP, a well-deserved recognition on one of the most incredible individual seasons in recent memory.

Hurts is also a model of consistency and could very well be on his way to a Hall of Fame career. His belief in consistency ignited when the Alabama Crimson Tide made consecutive College Football Playoff National Championship appearances in 2016 and 2017.

There's no doubt that the lessons he learned from Coach Nick Saban have shaped his mindset as a pro. Saban's approach at Alabama, "We don't practice until we get it right. We practice until we can't get it wrong," is the epitome of consistency, which is why, before the Eagles Super Bowl season in 2024, Hurts specifically cited sustainability and consistency as his goals for the season.

■ ■ ■

Armed with an overall understanding of why consistency is essential to your success, it's time to go deeper and explore the elements that contribute to executing tasks on a consistently high level.

As you read through the following, ask yourself if you possess these traits or what you can do to better integrate them into your life.

Peak-level time management. If you're wasting your time on things that don't matter, you are torpedoing your consistency efforts. You must keep asking yourself how you're spending time on various activities, putting you closer or driving you further away from what you want to accomplish. Without exception, everything you do falls into one category or the other. If you want to see a person's priorities, I say show me their calendar.

I'm a strong believer in the Pareto Principle, also known as the 80/20 rule, that says 80% of the outcomes come from 20% of your efforts. In other words, the most important 20% of what you do determines the outcomes for 80% of your life. Does your calendar reflect this?

Rinse and repeat mentality. Can you complete tasks over and over again at a high level? Can you learn and refine your efforts, and not let setbacks derail your efforts? You must be able to rinse away the doubts accompanying defeats, lock in on what comes next, and repeat your efforts with lessons learned from previous attempts.

Mastery of the mundane. Positive results from small, tedious tasks compound and often are the foundation for significant breakthroughs. If you don't do the boring little things well, you're building a house of cards that will collapse at critical times when you're working on the big goals in your life.

Incorporate discipline daily. You must make several things nonnegotiable as you strive for consistency. If you want to get fit, exercise every day. If you want to put a million dollars or more in the bank, work on high-value tasks that best advance your cause. Taking days off is sometimes necessary for balance in your life, but be strategic and recharge your batteries in ways that collaborate with your big-goal efforts.

Create standards. Just like discipline, standards are nonnegotiable. You can't always control wins and losses, but you can control the framework of how you approach your challenges. Standards are the guardrails that define processes and give you the best chances for success. They remove many decisions and emotions that can undermine your efforts in the heat of a battle.

An appreciation of the compounding effect. One of the core principles of wealth is setting aside a percentage of your income as early as you can in your career and letting time compound wealth over long periods. The compounding effect works in many business and personal situations as well. You advance toward your goals in small increments that add up over time. When you keep banking small accomplishments, eventually you'll wind up with a big bottom-line number.

Avoid comparisons. Keeping your blinders on like a horse in a race helps you avoid the unnecessary noise of what others are doing around you. Theodore Roosevelt summed it up nicely when he said, "Comparison is the thief of joy."

Distractions deter you from your plan and are counterproductive to your success. Comparison robs you of your greatness and provides no value, as your potential is limitless and still unfolding. Each of our uniqueness, gifted to us, comes together as an orchestra when we allow it. Remember, a trumpet doesn't compare itself to the drum.

Take action. This sounds obvious, but you'd be surprised by how many people are brilliant thinkers who do nothing but think, letting great opportunities slip away because they're paralyzed by overanalysis. To be successful, avoid paralysis by analysis by consistently being a great thinker *and* a great doer.

Be predictable. Some people see this as boring, but when you are predictable, others will rally to your known cause, helping you along the way. Others know better than to distract you from your laser-focused efforts, keeping your path clear and your distractions to a minimum.

Be organized. Your brain, business, and your personal workspace must be orderly to create consistency. If you're forever looking for something, or workers don't know their place in your overarching plans, you waste time and destroy momentum. Making this a core habit also minimizes unnecessary frustrations.

Add and subtract within your framework. Remain flexible, adding or removing people, processes, and unnecessary burdens that have grown stale or no longer serve your best efforts. Consistency doesn't mean staying the same. It means consistently reevaluating the elements of your framework to create the best outcomes.

Make your results measurable. Measuring your results provides valuable feedback. In turn, this increases your chances for success. This is more than looking at numbers to see what's working best in your life. It's about asking why and seeing if you can adopt those processes and standards on a broader scale.

Optimize tasks. Consistency is all about achieving results, and the way to get the best results is to break down tasks into their individual elements and study them to ensure they are the best solutions for optimal outcomes. One minor flaw in your processes can have a harmful ripple effect that can hold you back in several ways.

Assign clear rights and responsibilities. People who work for you can't consistently deliver their best results when they don't know what they're supposed to be doing. Part of this is ensuring you have the right people in the correct positions.

Give clear instructions and set clear expectations. Be clear about what people are responsible for and who they should report to directly. Set proper expectations and be consistently clear on outcomes.

Build an optimal infrastructure. People deliver consistently outstanding results when you give them the tools they need to perform at the highest levels. If inadequate resources or other barriers hamstring them, results and efforts will vary, sometimes significantly, undermining your big picture efforts.

Recruit the best talent. Talent loves the freedom to consistently explore new ways of doing things, often leading to breakthroughs and high levels of job satisfaction. To protect my culture, I weigh each potential new hire carefully. I am slow to hire but also quick to fire when there's not a good match in talent and attitude.

Attract fans and influencers to your cause. When you're consistent with your place in business, consistency becomes an important part of your brand. Repeating your message over and over helps you break through noise and clutter to attract a diverse set of supporters who will tell your stories in ways you can't always do.

■ ■ ■

Despite your best intentions, you may struggle with consistency. If so, you're not alone. As you've learned, many components are required to achieve a certain level of consistency. Don't beat yourself up if you're hit and miss with your efforts. The only way you lose in the consistency game is if you don't take time to analyze what's going on and then adjust your mindset and actions to raise your level of consistency.

Understanding why and where you fall short creates a blueprint for things you can work on for more consistent and higher-quality outcomes. Your shortcomings are unique to you, but several enemies of consistency are common across a broad spectrum of people.

For example, how many of the following do you struggle with?

Fear of failure

Unrealistic goals

Mental fatigue

Fear of change

Procrastination

Paralysis by analysis

Lack of motivation

Overcommitment

Negative self-talk

Negative talk to others

Lack of clear goals

Poor prioritization

Poor organization

Distractions

Lack of routine

Lack of clear communication

Stay on Track

The best way to minimize disruptions and distractions is to develop an accountability system and to use it to fuel your consistency efforts. I use an Activity Tracker that can tell me at a glance if I've hit my intermediate goals. Much like Seinfeld marking a calendar with big red Xs, this log is a highly effective way for me to stay focused.

 **Fall in Love with the Process**
Staying the course when pulled in many directions is the difference between making something optional or mandatory. We want mandatory success and results, but we treat the actions to get there as optional, wondering why the end result isn't what we had hoped. Only when we realize our actions must meet our ambitions to come true can we see the endless path of results we desire. Falling in love with the process, regardless of the process, is how we fall in love with the results of winning.

I spend a few minutes updating this tracker daily, but it's time well spent because I see incredible results when I do. It also helps me stay focused in a profession where it takes months to see income from my actions. When my goals are in black and white, and I put them in front of me routinely, I find it much easier to stay focused and consistent. There is no place to hide from the data, and in turn, this fuels my perseverance.

It's a lot like stepping on a bathroom scale daily when you're trying to lose weight. The scale doesn't lie. It is a simple way to keep you honest and focused on your goals.

I use the Activity Tracker that I showed you in Principle 2 and the Opportunity Tracker at the end of the chapter to document progress and keep myself accountable. The Lead Tracker is focused on how my activities convert into successful transactions, while the Opportunity Tracker is used for speed and responsive follow-up, which is where most people fall short. You can use the sample template below to create a system to track your efforts.

The Edison Approach

At the start of this chapter, I said that consistency is the purest form of perseverance. In that spirit, I want to share the story of a man who personified consistency in ways that continue to profoundly affect humanity today.

That man's name is Thomas Edison, widely considered the greatest inventor of all time. He had close to 1,100 patented inventions that advanced civilization. They were uniquely broad, ranging from electrical utility systems to recorded sound, motion pictures, alkaline storage batteries, figuring out the science behind the light bulb, and countless others. Edison also had another 500–600 patent applications that he either didn't finish or were rejected.

Much like Jerry Seinfeld, his pursuit of advancing his inventions resulted from insane curiosity and a consistent application of his best efforts. Throughout his life, Edison filled 4,000 notebooks that chronicled his life's work. His passion and inquisitiveness were legendary, even at an early age. As one story goes, when he was a child, Edison tried to solve the mystery of how and why eggs hatch by sitting on them in his brother-in-law's barn.

He was so disruptive and bored in school that his teachers ran out of patience, which eventually led to his mother taking him out of school and homeschooling him from an early age. Edison thrived because his ambition matched his curiosity.

While working as an employee of the Gold and Stock Telegraph Company, Edison invented the universal stock printer and received $40,000 for it. Using funds from that sale, he opened a factory in Newark, New Jersey, where he built stock tickers and poured his time and talents into other inventions. He was just 23 at the time.

Edison understood that focused thinking needed to be combined with taking action, which explains why his work ethic was legendary. He often rose at 4 a.m. and worked 18+ hours a day. Other times, he napped during the day and worked entirely through the night. Frequently, Edison would forget to eat and bathe because of his single-minded pursuit of his passions. Instead of resting on his accomplishments, each breakthrough excited him more, creating new questions and problems to solve, leading to new ways of thinking that often resulted in other dramatic scientific advancements.

Was Edison obsessive? Absolutely. Was he consistent in his single-minded pursuit? Without a doubt. Did he understand perseverance? Yes, with hundreds of documented examples. The best example of this was his 10-year process of attempting to invent the alkaline storage cell battery, during which he conducted 50,000 experiments to further his big goal.

Of course, Edison was one of a kind. You may not reach the same level of success, but we can still turn to him for valuable insights as one of the most important examples of consistency and perseverance the world has ever seen.

OPPORTUNITY TRACKER

Your Numbers & Metrics	January	Goal
LEAD TO CREDIT	63%	70%
CREDIT TO PRE APP	60%	50%
LEAD TO CLOSING	0%	25%
JANUARY LEADS		
Monthly Leads Goal 2025	40	
Monthly Leads Actual 2025	8	
OVER/UNDER - LEAD GOAL	-32	
JANUARY CREDIT PULLS		
Monthly Credit Pulls Goal 2025	28	
Monthly Credit Pulls Actual 2025	5	
OVER/UNDER CREDIT PULL PROJECTION	-23	
JANUARY PRE-APPROVALS		
Monthly Pre-Approvals (LT) 2025	3	
JANUARY LEAD TO PRE-APPROVAL %	38%	
JANUARY CLOSINGS		
Monthly Closing Goal 2025	10	
Monthly Closing Actual 2025	0	
OVER/UNDER CLOSING PROJECTION	-10	
PREVIOUS YEARS DATA INPUT (2024)		
Monthly Leads 2024		
Monthly Closings 2024		
2024 Lead to Closing %		
2025 LEAD ANALYSIS		
CCR	Current Client Referral	1	
PC	Past Client	1	
PR	Past Client Referral	1	
PF	Personal Friend	0	
RLTR	Realtor	3	
AD	Advertisement	0	
BUS	Business Partner	0	
BLDR	Builder	1	
TOTAL	7	

Name	PQ Status	Referral Source Name	Date	Credit Pulled	Pre-Approved	Closed	Source	Notes
Jane Doe	Purchase			Yes	Yes	FEB	BLDR	
Example	Refinance			Yes	No		PR	
Example	Purchase			Yes	Yes		RLTR	
Example	Purchase			Yes	No		RLTR	
Example	Refinance			No	No		RLTR	
Example	Purchase			Yes	Yes		CCR	
Example	Refinance			No	No		PC	
Totals								
8				5	3	0		

6

Creating Financial Security

I t's one thing to persevere. It's quite another to persevere with a purpose. For many people, one of the primary purposes of grinding and working hard for years is to accumulate significant wealth.

Wealth is only one way to keep score of how you're doing in life. But let's face it, for many people, it is *the* way to keep score. There's nothing wrong with that. I've been dead broke, and I now know what it's like to have financial freedom. I assure you that while some people bash capitalism and the pursuit of money, as much as anything else, it's how a big part of your quality of life is defined.

This is why you must develop a healthy relationship with money. Understand what it can do for you and, in some cases, what it can't. Obsessing about money is not healthy, but putting it to work for you so you can do good for others is.

If you are diligent and work hard, there may come a point in your life when you will feel safe and secure about how much money you have. That's a critical threshold to cross. In my case, that happened when I was in a room with my fellow coaches after a large event. It wasn't just that I had achieved a certain level of wealth that meant I never needed to work anymore. It was also about realizing I no longer needed to prove to my mom that I was worthy. This, even though she had been dead for 10 years!

While I was happy to reach that point, I wasn't completely satisfied because I still felt I needed to keep growing. It's an important distinction to make.

Looking back, there are two questions I had to answer to help me reach that place of safety.

The first was, "What would I tell the 17-year-old version of me in terms of how much money I need to feel safe?"

The second was, "Why was I pursuing financial security so intensely?"

It's one thing to chase money for the sake of purely gaining financial wealth. But to be truly wealthy, you must also answer the question of why you want to take on this difficult challenge. Knowing your purpose is the jet fuel that will get you through tough days when you want to quit or suffer a significant setback. It goes beyond motivation to a central core of who you are.

The best thing about thinking this way is that it removes much of the need for external validation and replaces it with an inward-facing determination you control. Answering both of these questions will raise your level of happiness, but still allow you to remain unsatisfied because you still want to grow.

Like anything else, you can learn how to make money. You must be focused, smart, and a lifelong student of financial education to grow your wealth over time. There are right and wrong ways, and while I can't cover all of them here, I understand that making money and making it work for you is all about playing the long game. In other words, growing wealth is all about perseverance.

Rich Dad Poor Dad author Robert Kiyosaki has a vast body of work on our relationship with money. His first rule is that the poor work for money while the rich put their money to work. It's part of the answer to the fundamental question, "Do you live to work or work to live?"

While many people love what they do, imagine having the freedom and the choice to choose what kind of work you want to do and doing it in a way that pays you well, so you can enjoy other parts of your life.

Kiyosaki also believes that parents and teachers focus on academic intelligence as essential, but not enough emphasis is placed on financial intelligence. In many cases, this is left up to you as an individual. That's surprising because you can be incredibly book smart, but what good is that if you can't translate it into making a good living? In his world, financial freedom is available to those who learn about it and work for it.

My boss and mentor is Ron Leonhardt, CEO of CrossCountry Mortgage. I've learned much from him about the mortgage loan industry and the right way to think about money and wealth.

One of the most important things he taught me is how to run my business the same way he runs his business, specifically, by paying attention to details that most people overlook. For example, the nickels and dimes are related to running expenses and revenues on a profit and loss statement. He also taught me how to lean in and scale up when your competitors are retreating. We could do this because we were diligent at all times, creating reserve funds we could deploy to take advantage of changing conditions.

I also learned a lot from my first coach, Josh Sigman. One of the most important things he taught me is that when you're paying off debt and investing simultaneously, put 50 cents of every dollar saved toward debt, then the other 50 cents toward investing to keep both moving in the right direction. Once the debt is completely paid, then the full dollar goes toward the investment. He also taught me that as you earn more, keep your lifestyle the same and increase the investment allocation. This is where many people fail because they usually only increase the quality of their lifestyle, and end up broke like I did.

Two Important Questions

Everyone wants financial security and independence. While no two paths to this goal are identical, you should answer some basic questions early in your quest to help you dial in your efforts. When I answered these questions, they helped me produce incredible results by clarifying what matters and why.

The two most important questions you should ask are the following:

What was your relationship with money
as a child?

Why do you want to be wealthy?

Why does the relationship with money as a child matter? Studies have shown that children between 8 and 12 years old are in the early stages of learning about money as part of the foundation of knowledge they'll need as adults. Often, opinions formed at this age become more ingrained over time. When a flawed relationship with money begins at an early age, it can influence all parts of your life for many years. For me, that meant a lot of days filled with agonizing highs, lows, and feelings of instability.

Once I answered these questions the right way, my wealth building took off. For me, the answers were a combination of basic survival early on and fear that I would fall into a hole of poverty that I would never climb out of. I wanted to be wealthy to overcome years of feeling worthless, fueled by a deep desire to prove naysayers wrong and to overcome my dysfunctional past that I documented in earlier chapters. Moving from surviving to wealth accumulation and ultimately to my legacy has taken years and will probably be with me for the rest of my life.

Reaching the Summit

So many people give up just before they reach the summit. For one reason or another, they abandon a perseverance mindset even though the triggering obstacle is a much worse outcome than the effort required to meet their biggest long-term goals.

Giving up before we start is one thing, but giving up just before we finish without knowing it is quite another. How many times have you done this in the past, finding out you were right there?! You experience feelings of regret and blame that linger when you don't stay the course and keep your blinders on until you reach your goal.

Your motivations and your relationship with money could be similar, but chances are they're not. There are many ways to have a healthy relationship with money, and several ways that are not. The same applies to why you want to be wealthy.

Understand that money is an amplifier of who you are. If you are frugal when you're poor, you'll remember what that feels like when your bottom-line wealth grows. Hopefully, you'll remain humble in how you use your money to improve your life and the lives of others you care about. If you have dreams of doing good in the world and are blessed with wealth, stay true to that belief as you combine it with providing security for your family, friends, and business associates.

I'm aware that my life could have turned out much differently, so I practice gratitude daily for my financial success. I also remind myself that money is only one measurement of how truly wealthy a person is. Some of the mentors who tried to teach me that money is everything turned out to be wrong. Now, I have a balanced approach to money, understanding its value but not letting it be the only thing I want in life.

I figured out long ago that true worth is not measured only by how much money you have in the bank but by how healthy and wealthy your soul is. In other words, the financial wealth I've reached on Earth is not the same as the wealth I achieve when praying or eventually going to heaven.

Although I've been a top-200 loan originator in the nation and built an eight-figure net worth in business, I'm still focused on lifting up others. I am paying forward my good fortune through mentoring, maintaining character in my personal and professional life, course correcting daily, and genuinely believing that working hard for my team and clients will make their lives better, as it has mine.

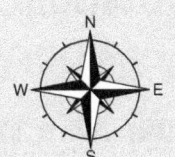 **Remove Dysfunctions**

What dysfunctions have you been using to falsely fuel your passion? We tend to hold onto things we know don't serve us because of their familiarity, even when it is toxic. You should ask yourself what dysfunctions you've been holding onto, because if you haven't figured it out yet, they are lies. Understanding what they are is critical to detaching from them going forward. They are holding you back, and removing them and the bad habits they create destroys false comforts you've sold yourself on as a necessity.

As I've reached these financial goals, my relationship with money has changed in some ways. I no longer feel the need to prove anything to my mom or anyone else. I no longer live in fear when it comes to attaining financial security. The frequency and the ways I worry about money have changed, but fundamentally, I still see money as an essential tool that helps me accomplish good things for myself and others. It's only later in life that I realize how important this shift has been as part of my success.

An Emotional vs. a Tactical Relationship with Money

To accumulate wealth, you must transition from an emotional to a tactical relationship with money. The emotional relationship is fueled by fear. As a result, emotions blind you to financial opportunities in the future. When you have an emotional relationship with money, you miss those opportunities or take the wrong ones because you're more focused on not losing than on winning.

The bottom line is that financial decisions driven by emotions often lead to financial failure and burnout.

Financial decisions driven by strategy are much more likely to lead to financial freedom.

Tactical relationships with money are fueled by education and opportunity. Understanding where and how to look for ways to tip the financial scales in your favor is how fortunes are made.

For example, buying real estate at the peak of a hot market in one part of the country doesn't make anywhere near as much sense as doing the hard work of researching emerging markets that offer the biggest upside for long-term appreciation.

Consider the following side-by-side comparison.

| EMOTIONAL vs. TACTICAL RELATIONSHIP WITH MONEY ||
Emotional Money Decisions	Tactical Money Decisions
Living paycheck to paycheck	Saving 20% monthly
Reckless spending without accountability	Following a detailed budget
Impulse purchases	No impulse purchase (sleep on it)
Short-term spending	Long-term investing
Short-term gains	Long-term gains
Only concerned with bottom line balance today	Understanding the value of compounding
Sell investments when they drop	Buy investments when they are on sale
Too afraid to make a profit	Not afraid to take a profit
Inconsistent investing and saving	Consistent investment and saving
Buy now – Pay later	Buy now – Pay now

Everyone has money triggers they must control. Just like a person with a sweet tooth always wants a piece of cake, a person without financial discipline who doesn't understand their triggers will always be broke. A lack of financial discipline is not strategic or tactical, it is emotional because it is selfish and short-term thinking.

You can still buy the things you want, but you must make conscious choices about what, when, and how much you'll spend *before* you whip out your wallet. Allotting a certain amount of your discretionary income to leisure activities, hobbies, and other pursuits is fine if you stay strict and don't eat more of that cake than you should.

Tactical relationships should be flexible as your situation changes. For example, as my income went up 30%, I shifted from autosaving 20% of my income to 50% of my income. The principles were the same when I was making $200,000 annually before I made the income jump to $1 million annually. I was disciplined because I was tactical, so I kept the same principles in place. I was building generational wealth and had the wisdom to never lose sight of that goal, unlike many others who spend a lot more when they make a lot more. Most people increase the quality of their lifestyle with income instead of making smart investments to pay for that lifestyle.

The Power of Budgeting and Compounding

Money should always be working, even while it sits.

That's a powerful truth often overlooked early in a person's relationship with money and building wealth. I was guilty of it, and I know many of you are just starting out to think the same way too.

Other than a few outliers like those who win the lottery or inherit wealth, you must master budgeting and understand the impact of compounding if you ever want to achieve financial success.

Consistency and Purity

Stay consistent in aligning your actions with your motives. Most of all, make sure those motives are pure in purpose, not selfish desires. When consistent actions and pure motives are aligned and repeated, we can accomplish what our inner voice won't always say is possible. Follow the process, make it a habit, and keep doing it even when you don't want to. Don't let others fall back into complacent reasons over results.

Budgeting is simple because it relies on one principle. That principle is discipline. What good is making a financial plan if you don't have the mental toughness to delay short-term gratification for a huge payoff further down the road? Understanding financial discipline is easy, but executing a disciplined plan is much harder. Most people lack discipline, which is why most people are not wealthy.

You must learn to budget and allocate your income the right way. That includes managing the essentials in your life, limiting or eliminating unnecessary purchases and commitments, and generally living below your means. You must also include setting aside a portion of your money for savings and investing, otherwise, you're not budgeting correctly. In that case, you're little more than a hamster running on a wheel in a cage, spinning furiously but not going anywhere.

People often fail at budgeting because they don't have a clear long-term goal of what they want to accomplish. They haven't answered the two key questions about money. Plus, they haven't gotten rid of their emotional attachment and switched to a tactical use of their money.

Budgeting is a fairly simple process after you've dealt with these issues. Until you do, your finances will leak like an old rudderless boat in a rocky ocean. You may survive the journey, but you won't like getting tossed about without a clear destination insight.

Compounding is a simple but powerful tool that is one of the most important weapons you can unlock over the long term. It can take many forms, but for our purposes, let's talk about its impact on your money.

Consider this. With compounding, you can either pay it in the form of interest on credit card debt or collect it month after month by investing it wisely. Albert Einstein said it best when he noted, "Compound interest is the eighth wonder of the world. He who understands it, earns it . . . he who doesn't, pays it."

When you set aside an initial fixed sum of money in an investment vehicle that grows and pays you over time, those payments stack up or compound each other. When you have the discipline to leave that money alone, it creates a larger baseline from which the money compounds, so payments grow larger more rapidly over time.

Here's another way to look at it. If you invest $100 a month over 40 years and earn an average 10% return, you could end up with a portfolio worth $531,000.

Even if you invested $1,000 one time as a young person and added nothing to it, at the end of 50 years, assuming an annual 10% growth, you'd have well over $100,000 banked.

COMPOUND INTEREST EXAMPLE $1,000 growing at 10% annually		
ELAPSED TIME	PORTFOLIO VALUE	GAIN IN PREVIOUS 5 YEARS
0	$1,000.00	N/A
5	$1,610.51	$610.51
10	$2,593.74	$983.23
15	$4,177.25	$1,583.51
20	$6,727.50	$2,550.25
25	$10,834.71	$4,107.21
30	$17,449.40	$6,614.69
35	$28,102.33	$10,652.93
40	$45,259.26	$17,156.93
45	$72,890.56	$27,631.30
50	$117,390.85	$44,500.29

If you want further evidence of the power of compounding, take a look at housing appreciation percentages since 1942. Real estate has always been a gold standard of long-term investing, and the next chart demonstrates why. It can be particularly dynamic during unprecedented growth, such as between 1943 and 1947, when prices rose 118%. After that, prices rose for the next 43 years, until 1990, when a slight 1% dip took place, followed by another 14 years of upward growth until 2007, when inventory far outweighed demand and we experienced a five-year correction.

Year	Nominal	Year	Nominal	Year	Nominal
1942	3%	1970	8%	1998	6%
1943	11%	1971	4%	1999	8%
1944	17%	1972	3%	2000	9%
1945	12%	1973	3%	2001	7%
1946	24%	1974	10%	2002	10%
1947	21%	1975	7%	2003	10%
1948	2%	1976	8%	2004	14%
1949	*0%*	1977	15%	2005	14%
1950	4%	1978	16%	2006	2%
1951	6%	1979	14%	2007	*-5%*
1952	4%	1980	7%	2008	*-12%*
1953	12%	1981	5%	2009	*-4%*
1954	1%	1982	1%	2010	*-4%*
1955	*0%*	1983	5%	2011	*-4%*
1956	1%	1984	5%	2012	6%
1957	3%	1985	7%	2013	11%
1958	1%	1986	10%	2014	5%
1959	*0%*	1987	8%	2015	5%
1960	1%	1988	7%	2016	5%
1961	1%	1989	4%	2017	6%
1962	*0%*	1990	*-1%*	2018	5%
1963	2%	1991	*0%*	2019	4%
1964	1%	1992	1%	2020	10%
1965	2%	1993	2%	2021	19%
1966	1%	1994	3%	2022	6%
1967	2%	1995	2%	2023	6.6%
1968	4%	1996	2%	2024	5.7%
1969	7%	1997	4%		

Only 7 out of 82 years since 1941 were down years, yet people trying to beat the market will outsmart themselves trying to time purchases when the housing market crashes. The fact is, housing, even when it dips, is a minor correction. People lose out when they don't understand compounding and appreciation, using historical data as a primary indicator of what to do with their money.

Having short-term and long-term goals helps you focus your budgeting and better understand how compounding can work for you.

For example, as I write this, my short-term goals include earning more passive income opportunities, making 50 or more connections a week, and making no large purchases for 12 months. For the long term, my goals are to invest 20–50% of my earnings every month for the rest of my life and build a $100 million real estate investment portfolio. This is a challenging goal for me and may change in the future. It's flexible because nobody should put a cap on their thinking, whether too big or too small. Always think big!

What Billionaires Can Teach You About Accumulating Wealth

Warren Buffett, Jeff Bezos, Oprah Winfrey, Elon Musk, and Larry Ellison.

They all started with little in life, but they have since become mega-affluent household names with a combined wealth of over a trillion dollars. There are other equally successful business rock stars, but these are the ones who have unlocked the secrets to creating stunning prosperity in a more public way than anyone else. They are studied, quoted, copied, and are a constant presence in the lives of the international business community. Their influence continues to define how business is done in all business sectors.

They all have something else in common. Each started in life with modest means and was raised in middle-class families. They did not inherit millions of dollars or have generational wealth passed down to them.

Their origin stories are well known. Jeff Bezos's parents were teenagers when he was born into a family of modest means, and he grew up working on his grandparents' ranch in Cotulla, Texas. Warren Buffett was born into a middle-class family in Omaha, Nebraska, and started delivering newspapers and selling golf balls and stamps.

Oprah Winfrey was born in rural Mississippi to a single teenage mother, was molested, and became pregnant at 14. Larry Ellison was also born to a single mother and given up for adoption when he was 9 months old.

All are self-made people who became billionaires through hard work, smart work, and fearlessly taking calculated risks to leverage opportunities they created for themselves.

You may not achieve the level of wealth they have, although you should never say never. What you can do is learn from the common traits these people displayed at an early age and continue to leverage throughout their public lives. You can model and mimic their character traits and the strategies they used to create tremendous wealth as you pursue your dreams of doing the same.

Thousands of books, podcasts, articles, and more have been devoted to studying these successful entrepreneurs to unlock their secrets. I encourage you to do the same if you're wired for financial success. My purpose is to start that conversation with you and within you so that you can add to your ongoing journey with some overarching wealth accumulation tactics.

Here are some of the traits these people have in common, and if you fold these things into your thinking, you'll be further along in charting a course for your financial independence.

Insane curiosity. From an early age, all sought answers to problems. That desire to learn has stayed with them throughout life. Each question they asked led to answers that have produced breakthroughs that have fundamentally changed parts of society as we know it today.

Bootstrapping. These people started with little more than great ideas, an iron-willed focus on success, and a refusal to give up, even when faced with failure many times over as part of their journey. All have had their moments, including Jeff Bezos and the now-famous photo of him sitting at a modest utility table and a single computer when he launched Amazon in 1999.

Growth mindset. Focused on how to solve problems and make money doing it. Finding a need and filling it better than anyone else. They are mega-disruptors. They don't simply break out of boxes; they build completely new ones that conform to their vision of how the world should be.

Confidence. An unmatched conviction in their vision. They could make decisions that not only disrupted the status quo but created entirely new industries and ways of doing things. They transferred their inspired vision to those who work for them.

Resilience. Despite their setbacks, they dusted themselves off and tried new things. Each set their egos aside to learn essential lessons from their failures, which they applied to their next ventures. They used calculated risk tolerance as a building block for the resilience they needed early on—the resilience that eventually helped them break through and succeed.

Compounded success. They didn't cash out on their early successes. They continued to build new things and stack wins on top of each other. Compounded successes are easily the best way to create bigger bottom lines.

Relentless work ethic. They tossed the clock and the calendar. These people are hypercompetitive, and while they love money, the thrill of winning also drives them. For example, Bezos displayed drive and aptitude at an early age, launching his first venture, the Dream Institute, to promote creative thinking in young students while in high school. Winfrey polished her craft early and landed a co-anchor job for a local evening news broadcast when she was only 19.

Paying it forward. After achieving tremendous wealth over an extended period, all of these people have been generous with their wealth, donating large sums to various charities and creating foundations to administer their efforts. This is part of building their legacy, which we will get into much more in the next chapter.

Add a willingness to take bold action, hyperaccountability in themselves and others, and courage, and you have a good idea of why these legends succeeded.

However, one more common thread exists among their legendary growth and success.

That thread is perseverance.

7

Building the Road to Your Legacy

The final perseverance principle has the potential to be the most satisfying of all, but because it takes decades to create, it also requires the most perseverance of all the principles we've covered.

It is never too early or late to seek answers that help you build a life that defines who you are and how you'll be remembered. It leads to an important question you must think about:

What do you want your legacy to be?

We all go through phases, some more impactful on us and the people we care about. These phases directly result from our choices and can lead us to transform everything about who we are.

Sometimes, we're aware of when these parts of our lives are taking place. Other times, we only become aware of their overall meaning and magnitude after we've had time to reflect. Understanding how they fit into our legacy can take months, years, or decades.

One of the goals of persevering over a lifetime is to make smart choices that positively impact our legacy in ways that align with who we are. We should also be mindful of how we want to be remembered for our contributions to our friends, family, and profession, and if the accomplishments are significant enough, by a broader part of society.

The Story of General William Lyon

If you live in Southern California, have served in the armed forces, or have had a career in the aviation or home building industries, you may have heard the name General William Lyon before.

When we talk about legacy, his is one of the finest examples I've ever seen, and his story is worth mentioning because it touches on so many key points of legacy building and perseverance that can teach you how to build your own.

I had the honor of meeting him once at his home, looking at his historic car collection. While we chatted about a few things, one of the things I remember most is how he started out as a kid selling newspapers. From an early age, he was never afraid to roll up his sleeves to finish the job. Still, despite his considerable accomplishments, he struck me as a humble and proud man. That's something you can't fake, and it helps to explain why he was so impactful in everything he did.

At the start of World War II, General Lyon attended University of Southern California but did not graduate, instead choosing to serve in the US Army Air Corps starting in 1943. He later flew 75 combat missions during his tour of duty in Korea in 1953. During his service, the general earned 17 military awards, including the Legion of Merit, Distinguished Flying Cross, Air Medal with two oak leaf clusters, and eventually became a major general commanding more than 200,000 reservists and overseeing a budget of $700 million before he retired in 1979.

For many, his military career alone would have cemented his legacy as a war hero and esteemed military commander. However, after returning from Korea in 1954, he formed the William Lyon Company, became a founding member of the Commercial Bank of California, and began building homes throughout Southern California. Over the next 40 years, Lyon and his combined companies built more than 100,000 homes, creating a legacy of providing homeownership for thousands of Californians. Late in his life, William Lyon Homes merged with Taylor Morrison Home Corporation, creating the nation's fifth largest publicly traded homebuilder.

He also made his mark in the aviation industry with fellow Orange County developer George Argyros. Together, they bought the airline AirCal and controlled it until it was sold to American Airlines several years later.

To further cement his legacy and tell his story, Lyon founded the Lyon Air Museum near John Wayne Airport in Orange County, where it remains a popular visitor destination. Lyon was also a noted philanthropist, donating to several causes and impacting the lives of countless others.

General Lyon was a disciplined man, but he had his soft spots, too. He loved cars, a passion I have in common with him. The difference is that while I had a collection of Hot Wheels growing up, he went from seeing actors driving Duesenbergs to owning one of the world's largest collections of fine automobiles, worth more than $50 million at one point. He even joked that once he got into collecting, those things got a little out of control. Interestingly enough, even his hobby of car collecting grew to be part of his legacy.

He worked into his nineties, and continues to be remembered fondly even after he died in 2020 at 97 years old, with an estimated net worth of more than

$650 million, according to the *Orange County Business Journal* at the time of his passing.

I've only touched on some of the highlights of his extraordinary life, but that is how a legacy is built. He combined hard work, exceptional relationships, a life-long growth mindset, kindness, and humility to become an example for us all.

How can you create your legacy? Let's break it down and start you on your own life's story.

The Building Blocks of Your Legacy

Many of you have taken it upon yourselves to write your 5-year plan, or perhaps you've thought about a 10-year plan. When we're in the middle of working hard, raising a family, and building wealth, it can be challenging to take a step back to think about life in even longer terms, but that's exactly what building a legacy is all about.

You don't have to be obsessed with life 20 or 30 years down the road. There are too many surprises, twists, and turns to try to control life to any measurable degree that is far down the road. However, I highly recommend having a general sense of what you want to accomplish and how you want to be remembered many years into the future. The best way to do that is to be aware of that timeframe while taking steps to do the best you can from day to day and year to year.

Practice Consistency Over Time

Planting seeds and expecting fruit to appear instantly is not reasonable, but today, it is expected in many areas of our lives. The speed at which life moves in some ways, from using microwaves and countless online retailers to banking and more, moves at a dizzying rate of speed. While these things are great tools for getting things done in a fraction of the time they used to take, the reality of personal growth is that it takes long, consistent periods of effort, discipline, and consistency over time.

Many people are impatient, and when they don't see immediate big-picture results, they give up and move on, often to something that gives them a short-term rush, but that doesn't move the needle much in their lives. For them, perseverance is still a ghost, a lesson yet to be learned, not understanding that those who persevere end up with a larger harvest than they ever imagined.

To create a positive and long-lasting legacy, there are several things you should consider incorporating into your life. It's fair to say that if you care about your legacy at all, it becomes more important the older you get. The key is to start by introducing elements to build and cement your legacy early on so they align with who you think you want to be later in life. One way to do this is to ask yourself if your future self will say thank you to your current self.

Legacy is built on vision, decisiveness, and sustained action. Like an apple tree, you must start building your legacy today to enjoy the fruits of your labor well into the future.

Here are some building blocks that are essential to focus on as part of your legacy-building efforts. They are general because we are all wired differently and have a unique path to find where we ultimately want to end up. These are thought starters, but it is up to you to reflect and incorporate things that are personally important to you as you guide yourself as part of your legacy-building efforts.

Understand your purpose. Knowing your real "why" and what drives you to create a lasting impact is crucial for building a legacy. My career and earnings soared once I combined my long-term why and how with my daily efforts. That harmony is crucial for success.

Vision and goals. Having a clear vision for what you want to achieve and setting actionable goals helps guide your actions toward building a legacy. You must move from your mind to paper and take action for these to be effective and ensure accountability. Visualize it and then act on it!

Continuous learning. Staying up-to-date and embracing new knowledge throughout life ensures your legacy remains relevant and impactful. The smartest among us are those who remain lifelong students.

Give back to the community. Actively contributing to your community through service, philanthropy, or mentorship can significantly shape your legacy. I fully believe God meant for us to serve others, and I live by that standard by paying it forward every chance I get.

Positive impact on others. Treating others with kindness, respect, and integrity builds a strong foundation for a positive legacy. The golden rule is so simple, although it is not always easy.

Do the right thing in your decision-making. Making choices aligned with your values and moral compass ensures your legacy is built on strong principles. It's not about who you were; it's about who you want to be. Whether through formal recognition, simple expressions of gratitude, or highlighting examples of good conduct, it encourages others to follow suit. Lock in your moral compass and revisit it often, like I do.

Mentorship and succession planning. Passing on knowledge and skills to future generations helps solidify your legacy. Show others the path you have already taken. We lift each other up as we climb mountains together.

Build relationships. Investing in meaningful connections with others can strengthen your legacy through your positive impact on their lives. Working with aligned friends who become a valued part of your inner circle is also more fun when everyone succeeds.

Put long-term value over short-term gains. In my experience, prioritizing quality over short-term gains has always been the key to sustainable success. For instance, when establishing my company, I focused on working with high-quality team members, even if it meant higher initial costs. This decision paid off in the long run, building a reputation for excellence, consistency, and client confidence. Spend wisely now so you can better cash in later. Also, saving on unnecessary burdens and expenses now is another way to enjoy more financial security later. When you don't, it shows.

Empower your team members to prioritize quality. Provide them with the resources, training, and autonomy they need to deliver exceptional products and services. Fostering a culture where quality is valued above all else ensures consistent excellence across all aspects of the business. That attention to quality doesn't always cost more, and in many cases, saves you money, time, and aggravation later.

Lead by example. As a leader, your actions should reflect the values of a strong work ethic, transparency, and doing the right thing. For instance, I make a point of always being transparent with our clients and team. I am a firm believer in accountability. I can be your friend sometimes, but I expect others to be accountable, too, no matter our personal or professional relationships.

Foster open communication. Creating an environment of open communication is essential for building trust. Encourage team members to voice their ideas, concerns, and feedback openly. In my experience, fostering open communication channels leads to innovative solutions and a stronger sense of community and unity within the team. Ask for ideas, seek focused feedback, and require honesty, even when it's difficult to hear. Be ready to take criticism to heart and be mindful of how you dish it out to others. Always consider feedback in any form as a gift. Most importantly, take action on that feedback.

Be generous with your resources. True wealth lies in generosity. Through philanthropy, businesses can make a meaningful impact, transcending personal ambition to empower communities. I am fully committed to the belief that the more you give, the more you are blessed. There will always be people in need, including your family, friends, employees, and strangers. It feels good to help others but be mindful of when that giving no longer feels good to you and redirect to a place where it does.

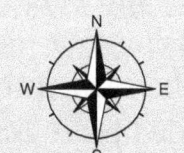

Assumptions vs. Reality

One cannot judge the past until the present unfolds what it really is. We make assumptions about what something means and find out we were wrong the whole time. Sometimes, we live in those assumptions for years until we truly understand. This understanding comes when we are ready and mature enough to accept what it truly is. The best we can do is not live in it, but let it stay where it was in the past until God shows us the lesson it was meant for. Then we can appreciate it, good, bad, or indifferent, for all its purpose and beauty, while not missing what's in the present.

Change Takes Time, But . . .

Change takes time, but it doesn't have to take a lifetime.

The journey from where we are today to where we want to be in the future can be daunting. It can be filled with challenges and opportunities. But in those challenges, we find the seeds of our own growth.

Let me tell you a real story reflecting a decade's transformative power.

Several years ago, a man I know struggled in a dark place. Bankrupt and living in a small, 1,000-square-foot home, he was pedaling his bike to a rented cubicle every day, staring at the wreckage of a failed career and feeling the weight of trying to be a good husband and father. His savings were depleted, and he had cashed out his 401(k) just to survive. To mask his pain, he turned to drinking and drugs, which only compounded his sense of shame, pain, and fear. He was lost and felt no purpose in his work or this world, utterly disconnected from his faith and burdened by a sense of brokenness.

But in his heart, he held a tiny flicker of hope. He made a promise to himself that things would change. Day by day, he worked to rebuild what was shattered, challenging himself to push beyond the limits he had unknowingly placed on himself. He knew that to rise above, he had to exceed his expectations. He began investing in his personal growth and facing his fears head-on, taking each setback as an opportunity to learn and improve.

Today, his story is a testament to the power of perseverance and belief. This individual now has a net worth of tens of millions of dollars and runs an eight-figure annual revenue business with over 20 locations and a team of over 100 members. His relationship with his wife has transformed into something beautiful, full of love and mutual respect. He can live without financial fear with his 401(k) rebuilt and enough cash to retire. He now owns multiple dream homes and is firmly rooted in his faith. Purpose and accountability define his every step going forward, and he has found profound gratitude in every corner of his life.

This transformation wasn't miraculous. It resulted from consistent, dedicated effort, leaning into God and his faith, a willingness to confront and move beyond his fears, and a belief in his potential to exceed the expectations he had set for himself using the principles laid out in this book.

In case you haven't figured it out yet, that man is me.

Many of you are capable of an equally miraculous story. I know this because we are the same in many ways, with similar challenging circumstances and hurdles to overcome. You must persevere through all of it because you're the best person to remove the ceilings that others have put up.

■ ■ ■

Right now, I want you to reflect on your legacy journey. What do your 5- and 10-year plans look like? Have you thought much, if at all, about your potential legacy? Those pages may be written to some degree already. However, like all great writing, you can edit everything about your direction and standards going forward.

You have the power to reshape your future, break free from the constraints of today, and build a life beyond what you think you are capable of at this moment. Don't settle for less than what you are truly capable of achieving. Be bold in your vision and unyielding in your pursuit. I am the perfect example that anyone can rebuild, heal, and thrive if they fully commit their mind and effort to change a story that does not serve them well. I did it, and so can you.

May you find the courage to challenge yourself, exceed your expectations, and embrace the incredible potential for a meaningful legacy that lies within you.

Perseverance as a Way of Life

Your ability to persevere is unique to you because you're emotionally wired like no other person from the moment you are born. While I've told you about situations in which perseverance played a key role in my life, your experience with perseverance and how you respond are things you'll need to own in your unique way.

By now, I hope you've embraced the goals I set out at the beginning of this book. I wanted to make you aware of how perseverance can help you with the challenges in your life. You cannot escape these challenges. In fact, you should embrace them and figure out how to use them to your advantage and help you grow in all parts of your life.

Another goal was to give you perseverance strategies you can use to improve your life. For me, that strategy is practicing my faith not just with prayer but through my actions. It's more than just treating other people well. Faith is what allows me to treat myself well. Figure out what you're passionate about and use that as fuel to help you overcome short- and long-term obstacles.

One day, many years from now, you will look back on your life. At some point, you'll probably tally your wins and losses, right and wrong moves, and find that while you may have a few regrets, you discovered your best life because you persevered. I hope you can look back with pride at how you handled situations with grace, restraint, and kindness.

I also hope you develop deep and meaningful relationships based on respect and love. Relationships are rarely perfect, but when you persevere, you give them the chance they need to grow into something special.

As I developed a more finely tuned sense of perseverance, one of the biggest things that changed for me was the amount of gratitude I felt in my life. Part of this came from redefining my relationship with God and my faith. One of the byproducts of this change, when combined with a perseverance mindset, is that gratitude has become a natural part of who I am now.

Gratitude removes many of life's frustrations. As I've already mentioned, you can't be mad and glad at the same time. It is a reminder that, despite whatever you're facing, those challenges were put in your life for a reason. It's up to you to figure out what those challenges are and remind yourself of the reason they exist. When you find these answers, often you will understand that the perseverance you're frequently required to live with is a blessing, and blessings are a form of gratitude.

Without challenges in our lives, there is rarely pain and change leading to growth. As I've demonstrated and proven through the success I've enjoyed later in life, the biggest challenges are often accompanied by the most significant rewards. But this can't happen without a perseverance mindset.

The rewards waiting for you can't happen without being a servant of something bigger than yourself and also taking charge of your life and practicing self-leadership. If you can't be honest and hold yourself accountable for your actions, you have no chance of becoming the leader of your own life.

Do not think things to death. If you're not driving things forward, someone or something else is. You can talk yourself out of your best life quite easily if you're not willing to face facts and take bold steps. You must consistently take the right steps, time and again, to create habits that serve your purpose. Get it straight in your head that your purpose is far bigger than any paycheck. Also, remember that dreams and goals without actions are just thoughts, and indecisions are decisions made for us instead of taking ownership of our own lives.

When you apply these thoughts and strategies effectively, you will become wealthier than you are today, not just by the size of your bank accounts, the quality of your relationships, and material wealth, but also richer in emotional and spiritual wealth.

Over the long term, you will start thinking differently, including how you want to be thought of for generations. Building your legacy is demanding but rewarding work and can only be accomplished over a lifetime of kindness, consideration, and service to others. This is another form of gratitude for all the gifts that you have been given.

Sharing those gifts with others after a lifetime of overcoming challenges and succeeding through perseverance means you have lived a good life. And ultimately, that is the most that anyone can hope for.

Acknowledgments

No one climbs alone. This book—and the life behind it—wouldn't exist without the people who pushed, challenged, and believed in me along the way. You helped shape who I am as a leader, coach, father, husband, and man.

First and foremost, to **God**—through Christ, all things are possible. Thank You for being the source of every step and every second chance.

To **Bret Colson**—your creativity and care helped turn this idea into something real.

To **Josh Sigman**, my first coach—thank you for showing me how to scale with intention and raising my ceiling before I even knew one existed.

To **Ben Newman**—your fire, accountability, and relentless standard pushed me further than you'll ever know.

To **Rick Ruby and Todd Scrima**—your clarity and no-BS wisdom built the foundation I still stand on.

To **Tom Ferry**—thank you for helping me think bigger.

To **Rene Rodriguez**—thank you for helping me slow down, think deeper, and lead with purpose.

To **Ron Leonhardt**—your belief gave this dream wings.

To **Rory Vaden** and **Elle Kogler**—thank you for sharpening the vision and elevating the brand beyond what I imagined.

To **Roy Mason** and **Pastor John Randall**—your spiritual guidance has kept me rooted in what matters most.

To **Jessica Uphoff**—thank you for introducing me to a life-changing support system.

To my **CrossCountry team**—your grit, loyalty, and commitment are the heartbeat of this journey. I could never thank you enough.

To the **Impact Elite Coaching family**—especially **Josh**, **Gavin**, and **Haley**—thank you for building something bigger than business. It's legacy.

To the friends and mentors who continue to pour into me—

Brad Noubakht and **Hunter Marckwardt**, my brothers from another mother—thank you for your steady wisdom and loyalty.

Lisa Wells and **Niki Salter**—your honesty and heart always bring me back to center.

Jeremy Forcier—you make growth lighter and life richer.

Dave Savage—your generosity and collaboration lift us all.

Jim Reed—your directness has shaped me more than you know.

To every person I've coached or coached with—iron sharpens iron. You've challenged me, refined me, and helped me become more.

To lifelong friends like **Woody, Greg, Sue, Jimmy**, and so many others—thank you for sticking around through all the wild chapters.

To **Rick** and **Ron**—you've been like older brothers, steady with strength and wisdom.

To **Sam, Jenn**, and **Tiffany**—you have kept everything moving. I couldn't do a day without you.

To **Rachelle, Jessica, Lana, Aunt Jodie**, and **Jenna**—the family who's stood by me with love that words can't touch.

Finally, I want honor and remember those people who have passed from my world. Although you are gone, you are not forgotten.

This isn't just my story—it's all of ours.

About the Author

JJ Mazzo is widely regarded as a transformative coach who fuels growth through grit, perseverance, and purpose.

A decorated entrepreneur and eight-figure business owner, JJ built multiple income streams after overcoming one of life's greatest financial setbacks—filing for bankruptcy at 32 and becoming a multimillionaire by 37. His story is one of relentless determination, resilience, and reinvention. As one of the highest-producing mortgage leaders in history—surpassing billions in funded volume—JJ has become a symbol of triumph over adversity and a beacon for those seeking financial freedom.

He has authored numerous articles as a Forbes Coaches Council member and currently serves as a producing Executive Vice President at CrossCountry Mortgage with The Mazzo Group. JJ is also the cofounder of Impact Coaching and Training, an elite leadership development company launched in 2024 alongside other top industry professionals. Previously, he served for over a decade as a senior coach and director at The Core Training, retiring in 2023 after cementing his legacy in mortgage coaching.

Throughout his career, JJ has consistently ranked among the top 1% of mortgage originators nationwide and has been recognized as one of Orange County's premier mortgage bankers.

JJ lives in San Juan Capistrano, California, with his wife and two daughters. He is an active member of the Orange County Association of Realtors and serves on the board of First Home IQ. He is also a proud supporter of the Children's Hospital of Orange County, the Orange County Rescue Mission, and Giveback Homes—organizations that align with his passion for giving underserved families access to safe and secure housing.

Index

Perseverance Principles Tools & Resources Hub

Download your complimentary toolkit of forms, coaching guides, and implementation tools mentioned throughout the book. These resources are designed to help you immediately apply what you learn and start seeing results in your pipeline.

Your breakthrough is waiting. The question isn't whether you have what it takes—it's whether you're ready to discover the strength you already possess.

Ready to Level Up?

Download the Toolkit Now

Visit PerseverancePrinciples.com/Resources

66

A Personal Message from the Author

"I wrote Perseverance Principles not just to inspire, but to give you real, practical tools to overcome challenges and succeed. I've walked the tough road—and I want you to walk it with more clarity, confidence, and purpose. Download these tools today and take the first step toward building the life and legacy you're meant for!"

JJ Mazzo

99

 @jjmazzo_   Linkedin.com/in/jjmazzo